TESTIMONIALS FO...
TO HIGH P...

"Managing culture might be t...........ост part of a manager's job. In this actionable book, seven leaders share their lessons of experience about creating workplaces where people are empowered to excel, find meaning, build trust, and drive change without sacrificing their well-being along the way."

**—Adam Grant, *New York Times* bestselling author of
GIVE AND TAKE, ORIGINALS,
and *OPTION B* with Sheryl Sandberg**

"In a era of mass employee disengagement (like now!), this book may well provide answers many leaders are searching for!"

—Joost Minnaar, Co-Founder Corporate Rebels

"*From Hierarchy to High Performance* is a must-read for managers who know that a highly effective organization is essential for keeping pace with the challenges of accelerating change. Filled with practical examples and concrete practices, the authors give managers a valuable orientation for moving beyond the command-and-control management model. This book is a primer on the new ways of thinking and acting that are the foundation for creating a happy, healthy, and highly engaged workplace. Leaders of all levels who are serious about building nimble and responsive organizations will find this book a welcome companion."

**—Rod Collins, author of *Wiki Management:
A Revolutionary New Model for a Rapidly
Changing and Collaborative World***

"This book is compulsory reading for all those who want to change something in their organizations because they consider the status quo unsatisfactory or unhealthy for the people who work there, but also for the organization itself."

—Prof. Franz Röösli, Ph.D., Head of Center for Enterprise Development at University of Applied Sciences Zurich and core team member of the Beyond Budgeting Round Table (BBRT)

"*From Hierarchy to High Performance* is a powerful book for any manager or leader who wants to transform their culture. Each author brings their expertise, insights and wisdom with practical tools and steps to cultivate a workplace that promotes employees bringing their passion for the work and strengths while still making a profit, a delicate yet worthwhile balance."

—Michelle Burke, CEO of Energy Catalyst Group and author of *15 Minute Pause; A Radical Reboot for Busy People*

"There's a revolution occurring underneath all our feet — a 21st century, bottom-up shift from bureaucratic rule to valued human experiences. *From Hierarchy to High Performance* powerfully, simply, and boldly guides us through this revolution. A must-read for all transformational leaders!"

—Bill Jensen, author of *Future Strong* and *Simplicity*

"This collection, from true change agents and thought leaders, provides us with the most practical and leading-edge strategies, concepts and tools for changing culture in today's fast-paced organizations. A must read for all leaders, consultants and coaches."

—**Mark Samuel - CEO of IMPAQ and Author of *B STATE: A New Roadmap for Bold Leadership, Brave Culture and Breakthrough Results!***

"Almost anybody interested in high performance in the workplace will find something of interest here in this highly readable book."

—**Henry DeVries, author of the international bestseller *How to Close a Deal Like Warren Buffett* and *Persuade With a Story!***

"Innovative and inspiring! In a time where we now know we need a different kind of leadership, *From Hierarchy to High Performance* creates high performing organizations by giving people their voice and their life back. Exploring the qualities we can all possess as leaders *From Hierarchy to High Performance* creates the end of command-control and hails in the age of high performance participation and collaboration."

—**Teresa de Grosbois, #1 International bestselling author of *Mass Influence - the habits of the highly influential,* Chair - Evolutionary Business Council**

"Many are talking in general terms about the future of work, but this remarkably insightful set of perspectives is a must read for anyone trying to take workforce change and turn it to an advantage for their organization. This powerful and important book puts workplace change into vivid perspective and offers remarkably constructive ideas and thinking that will transform the effectiveness of organizations."

—**Jim Nichols, CMO Partnerize**

"Today's market and workforce conditions require organizational leaders to find new ways to release the potential of their people. *From Hierarchy to High Performance* is a great place to start looking."

—Timm J. Esque, Founder and Managing Partner, Ensemble Management Consulting, creator of Commitment-Based Project Management (CBPM), and author of *No Surprises Project Management.*

"*From Hierarchy to High Performance* is a "business" book unlike any other I have ever read. It was written by an incredibly diverse group of very smart people, each of whom has a compelling vision of a world that doesn't exist - yet. They offer specific guidance about how to transform highly-structured, bureaucratic, spirit-killing organizations into agile, caring, high-performing communities. Get a copy today, and become a transformational leader. It's easier than you can imagine."

—James Ware, PhD, Managing Editor, Work&Place and author of *Making Meetings Matter: Leading Collaborative Conversations in the Digital Age*

"The frameworks around business creation and how we accomplish work have forever been based on continuous evolutions of the past. However the authors behind *From Hierarchy To High Performance*, break new ground writing the rules for organizational success in the fast pace world of global business and remote team for today and beyond. As an entrepreneur, executive or leader of any sorts, this is your ultimate guide towards building a successful and sustainable organization."

—Kyle Ellicott, Founder ReadWrite Labs

"A focused work targeting C-level challenges with solutions based on real-world experience. This short and inspiring effort makes a quick read for long-term success!"

—Don Schmincke:
Best-Selling Author/Researcher/Speaker

"If you want to infuse more meaning and purpose into your workplace, read *From Hierarchy to High Performance*. This book provides practical advice for any leader who wants to create a tribe of True Believers."

—Lisa Earle McLeod, Bestselling author
of *Selling with Noble Purpose*

FROM HIERARCHY TO HIGH-PERFORMANCE

UNLEASHING THE HIDDEN SUPERPOWERS OF ORDINARY PEOPLE TO REALIZE EXTRAORDINARY RESULTS

AUTHORS:
DOUG KIRKPATRICK, BILL SANDERS,
DAWNA JONES, OZLEM BROOKE EROL,
JOSH LEVINE, SUE BINGHAM,
ANNA MCGRATH

Smart Hustle Publishing, LP
www.smarthustleagency.com

Copyright © 2018 Doug Kirkpatrick, Bill Sanders, Dawna Jones, Ozlem Brooke Erol, Josh Levine, Sue Bingham, Anna McGrath

All Rights Reserved

Paperback ISBN: 978-1-64184-032-3
Ebook ISBN: 978-1-64184-026-2

BUS097000   BUSINESS & ECONOMICS / Workplace Culture
BUS071000   BUSINESS & ECONOMICS / Leadership
BUS085000   BUSINESS & ECONOMICS / Organizational Behavior

DEDICATION

For those brave individuals striving to transform themselves, their teams and companies for the better.

TABLE OF CONTENTS

ACKNOWLEDGEMENTS

The list of people who have influenced the formation of Great Workplace Cultures starts with Joan Blades whose vision and optimism for a workplace characterized by trust and empowerment continues to inspire us. Rod Collins has been a faithful contributor, friend, and team member. We owe Annie Snowbarger much gratitude for her attention to detail and tireless dedication. Our cover design was generously contributed by Godfrey Dadich Partners whose outstanding design sensibilities achieved the seemingly impossible. We are grateful for the contributions of our publisher, Lisa Williams and appreciate her commitment to multi-author projects. Donna Mosher's contributions as editor were enormously practical; we felt like she really "got us" which made the process synergistic. Finally, to each of our respective professional networks and clients who are dedicated to making workplaces healthier and better for the economy and society.

FOREWORD

by Joan Blades, MomsRising

I first became an advocate for the opportunities to dramatically improve work for employers and workers as a co-founder of MomsRising.org. MomsRising is a grassroots organization working to achieve economic security for all moms, women, and families in the United States. It turns out that pretty much all the practices that are good for mothers are good for everyone. When work structures and practices fit the modern workforce, everyone wins. Employees are happier and more productive, and employers have a more loyal and resilient workforce. The result is nothing less than a stronger bottom line.

The contributors to this book are brilliant innovators and leaders who know how to structure workplaces that sing! If you have doubts about the need for improving work cultures, take a look at the data showing how disengaged the average worker is. Most workplace productivity is a fraction of what it could be. The happy news is this: workplace environments that are deeply respectful of all workers are also wonderfully productive. And, not surprisingly, they experience very low turnover.

So why don't employers take advantage of the opportunities to make people happier and improve profitability?

Most organizations don't change until they must confront a crisis. Leading change requires stepping into new territory, trying things, experiencing failures as well as successes, and contending with people who don't like change. The reward for leaning into change is an agile workforce of exceptional trust and shared purpose. It is a joy to be part of the happiness and productivity in a workplace where everyone brings their full capacity to their work. Creating a culture with this level of engagement is a practice—like staying fit or going to church, and it requires ongoing commitment.

As you read this book, consider if just maybe your workplace could be one of your favorite places to go.

You will gain insight, tools, and fresh perspective as you choose your path forward in your career, and in how you lead. Most importantly, you can decide if you fear or trust in human potential and how you want to contribute to that emotional tone in the future of work.

THE MOMENTUM OF CHANGE

by Bill Sanders, Roebling Strauss, Inc.

People don't fear change. In the US alone, people spend over $80 billion annually on lottery tickets that they hope will change their lives wholesale.[1] What people do fear is the unknown, uncertainty, and the loss of power, position and prestige.

The world is changing at an ever-increasing rate. Open any newspaper or tune into any newscast, and you can find all the evidence you need. Formerly, new products displaced old products; now, new business models are replacing entire industries. New tools, new programs, and new solutions arise every day. Some fail, some succeed, and as a whole, the flood of change sweeps away the old tools, programs, and solutions.

Yet every decision that an individual makes is a raindrop that helps create that flood. Eat out, or eat in; upgrade to the latest smartphone, or stay with the current model; stay in our current position or take a risk with a new one; our

---

[1]   "State lotteries: sales U.S. 2016 | Statistic." Statista. Accessed January 12, 2018 https://www.statista.com/statistics/215265/sales-of-us-state-and-provincial-lotteries.

decisions, in conjunction with those of millions of others, help accelerate change.

That acceleration, the pace of change, cuts both ways. In addition to ushering in the new, it is also democratizing information and rapidly eroding the foundations of our existing corporate structures. The resulting disruption and uncertainty are only going to increase, demanding that we create more flexible models for how we work.

Three primary drivers have aligned to fuel this acceleration:

- Technological Innovation
- Infrastructure and Access
- Evolving Culture

TECHNOLOGICAL INNOVATION

The speed at which technology advances is primarily determined by the speed at which we exchange and process information.
- Paul Zane Pilzer[2]

Innovation begets innovation. Uber, for example, could not exist without the invention of the smartphone by Apple. It's an example of digital convergence. And we haven't seen anything yet. What innovations will we see as artificial intelligence, blockchain, robotics, voice search, the Internet of Things, and self-driving cars proliferate and cross-pollinate?

Ronald Coase was awarded the Nobel Memorial Prize in Economic Sciences in 1991 primarily based on two

---

[2]   Paul Zane Pilzer, *Unlimited Wealth: The Theory and Practice of Economic Alchemy*, (New York, Crown Publishers, 1990), 15.

essays. One of those, "The Nature of the Firm," penned in 1937, explains why the corporation exists. He identified high "transaction costs" as the key driver in the creation of the firm. In short, companies are formed when the costs of transacting business, that is the costs of identifying, negotiating, and contracting with other individuals or companies, exceed the organizing costs, the costs of organizing and running a company.

Technological innovation through the process of digital convergence is now having a sustained impact upon that equation. Consider Uber's impact on the taxi industry. In 2014 a New York City taxi medallion, the right to operate a taxi, was worth $1.2 million. Now they are worth less than half of that, with some going for less than $200,000. This implosion has decimated the lending companies set up to support the industry as well, with three lenders already forced into receivership.[3]

Technological innovation is rapidly eroding the traditional barriers to entry into incumbent industries—capital, knowledge, and infrastructure. New ways of connecting people to services are providing insurgent companies and entrepreneurs the ability to quickly end-run the old models. And we are seeing only the beginning of this disruption.

INFRASTRUCTURE AND ACCESS

The technological innovation, however, needs distribution to gain critical mass, and that distribution is rapidly becoming ubiquitous. In November 2016, Pew Research Center found that 88 percent of Americans now use the internet,

---

[3]   CNBC. "Uber and Lyft have been so disruptive to NYC's taxi industry, they are causing lenders to fail." CNBC. July 15, 2017. Accessed January 12, 2018. https://www.cnbc.com/2017/07/15/uber-lyft-take-down-not-just-cab-drivers-but-also-lenders.html.

with broadband penetration at 73 percent and smartphone ownership at 77 percent.[4]

That is a fantastic level of adoption considering that Apple introduced the first smartphone just over ten years ago! Think about that for a moment. Nearly 80 percent of us own a pocket-sized computer with more computing power than IBM's Deep Blue supercomputer had when it beat Chess Grandmaster Bobby Fisher in 1997.[5] And at a mere fraction of the cost.

With the exception of very sparsely populated areas, one is rarely far from a cell phone signal in the US. This level of access to information, people, weather, and other tools is unprecedented in human history, and it is only going to increase.

EVOLVING CULTURE

When Henry Ford invented the assembly line, he did so in a quest for production speed, quality, and predictability. Mass production requires uniformity. The hole must be drilled the same way every time. The manufacturing tolerances must be the same for each part if they are to be interchangeable.

Mass production is about as far from bespoke and handmade as an industry can get, and it demanded a management system that could strip out much of the ambiguity of work. It's no wonder, then, that Fredrick Taylor's scientific management theory was so quickly adopted in the early twentieth

---

[4]   "Pew: U.S. Smartphone Ownership, Broadband Penetration Reached Record Levels in 2016." Telecompetitor. Accessed January 12, 2018. http://www.telecompetitor.com/pew-u-s-smartphone-ownership-broadband-penetration-reached-record-levels-in-2016/

[5]   "Your smartphone is millions of times more powerful than all of NASA's combined computing in 1969." ZME Science. September 10, 2017. Accessed January 12, 2018. https://www.zmescience.com/research/technology/smartphone-power-compared-to-apollo-432/

century. Designed to increase efficiency and productivity in the factory, scientific management helped drive the creation of our prevailing work structure. Scientific management and its derivative philosophies required increased management oversight and direction of employees. It resulted in more centralized decision-making and less autonomy for the rank-and-file worker.

Because it was successful in driving increased productivity, quality, and uniformity, it is unsurprising that many of the alternative approaches, like those of Mary Parker Follett, were largely ignored. As Peter Drucker put it in his introduction to *Mary Parker Follett: Prophet of Management*, "What she had to say, the 1930s and 1940s simply did not hear and, equally important, did not *want* to hear.[6] This holds true for every one of the four central postulates of Follett's management work."

Ms. Follett's four central postulates were as follows:

1. Conflict can be constructive. By seeking to understand the viewpoint and underlying concerns of an opposing side, we can uncover and create innovative solutions to seemingly intractable problems.

2. Management is not the sole domain of business, but a basic function required of non-profits and government agencies alike.

3. Management is a function rather than a set of tools.

---

[6] Follett, Mary Parker, and Pauline Graham. *Mary Parker Follett--prophet of management: a celebration of writings from the 1920s.* District of Columbia: Beard Books, 2003., 4. (Emphasis in the original.)

4. Citizenship must be reinvented, empowering individuals to become better citizens, since "nothing can work unless it is based on a functioning civil society."[7]

While all of these ideas are evident in management practice today, they were anathema to the existing structures and beliefs of the 1930s and 1940s. Our culture has evolved alongside our technological and economic advances and will continue to do so. How it evolves, and how quickly, is up to us.

THE FUTURE IS HERE

The future is here, it's just not evenly distributed.[8]
– William Gibson

Many of the underlying ideas circulating in the current conversation about the future of work have been here for decades, if not centuries. But only now have the economic forces, structures, and mindsets changed enough to begin to experiment with new ways of working.

We are in the early stages of the digital transformation, and the acceleration of that transformation is both terrifying and exciting. It is terrifying because it is a destabilizing influence: it increases uncertainty and ambiguity and challenges our long-held assumptions and expectations, eroding the confidence in our hard-earned skills and experience. And yet digital transformation is exciting because there's never been more opportunity to experiment, to create new

---

[7] Follett, and Graham, "Mary Parker Follett," 8
[8] "William Gibson." William Gibson - Wikiquote. Accessed January 12, 2018. https://en.wikiquote.org/wiki/William_Gibson

business models without requiring large amounts of capital, and to shape the next epoch of work.

The future cannot be predicted,
but futures can be invented.
- Dennis Gabor [9]

The disruption to our current economic system is only going to accelerate until we replace it with new approaches that help us adapt and thrive in the new environment. That process is messy and will negatively impact a high number of people who depend on the current economic system for their sustenance. As a consequence, we have a moral imperative to find our way to new systems as quickly as possible and to ease the economic impact of that transition.

Whether you are an employee, a manager, or an owner, you have a role to play. Here are three things you can do to prepare and contribute to the future of work:

1: Address Your View of Adversity and Failure

In a turbulent economy where the rules seem to be changing every day, our skills and expectations are continually being put to the test. Marshall Goldsmith proved prophetic when he named one of his books *What Got You Here Won't Get You There*.[10] Especially regarding the function of management, what got us here will not suffice to help us invent the future. Creating the future is going to require risk and experimentation, most of which will fail. Just as with innovation, our

---

[9]   Quote Investigator. Accessed January 12, 2018
       https://quoteinvestigator.com/2012/09/27/invent-the-future/
[10]   Goldsmith, M. (2008). *What Got You Here Won't Get You There: How Successful People Become Even More Successful*. Profile Books.

ability to achieve our desired outcomes is directly related to how quickly we can test and cycle through new approaches.

The key to testing and cycling quickly through new approaches is in how we view adversity and failure. Resisting change and challenges does not serve us. Conflict is not inherently harmful—whether it is conflict between people, conflict with policies and procedures, or simply obstacles preventing us from achieving our desired outcome.

Just as a bodybuilder lifts weights to increase their strength, we must embrace adversity and resolve its accompanying challenges if we want to increase our leadership skills. Sure, it would be nice if everything ran smoothly. If we had no challenges, it would be easier to meet our objectives, grow our businesses, or get promoted earlier. But what happens when difficult situations arise later, when you have more responsibility, when more is at stake? Especially if you haven't honed your skills at resolving those issues when there was less pressure.

Economic turbulence is accelerating at a rate greater than ever before in recorded human history. If you want to lead that change instead of being swept along by it, you must embrace adversity and use it to develop your skills. People who overcome adversity and achieve their objectives are rewarded with increasing levels of responsibility. And with increasing levels of responsibility come new levels of difficulty. This is why the skill you gain by overcoming the myriad of problems you must face to achieve your objectives is more valuable than the success itself.

We must address our view of failure as well. To be specific, I'm not talking about failure to complete a known task; I'm referring to efforts to innovate and improve. Failure, in this case, is merely an experiment that didn't produce the desired outcome. We are venturing into entirely new territory. An approach that asks, "What did we learn from this?" regardless of the "success" or "failure" of the attempt enables us to take our learnings and accelerate our own growth and our ability to cycle through the next round of experiments.

2: EDUCATE YOURSELF ON THE TRENDS, TOOLS, AND PRINCIPLES

You must educate yourself on the trends, tools, and principles that are being developed, discussed, and practiced by practitioners and innovators who are actively contributing to the "future of work." This book is a great start. In it, you are going to hear from Dawna Jones on the hidden cost of employee disengagement. Ozlem Brooke Erol explains why having purpose at work is so critical. Josh Levine delves into how to develop and maintain good relationships and an organization's culture as it grows so you can maintain "true north." Sue Bingham writes about the importance of trust and how to restore it to the workplace.

You'll also hear from Doug Kirkpatrick on why self-management is not just a trend, but the future of engaging talented people. And Anna McGrath shares ways to build your whole-body wisdom as well as choosing conscious (versus unconscious) commitments to grow what she calls your response-agility capacities.

3: EXPERIMENT AND TAKE RISKS

No matter what your role, you can begin to shape the future, even if it is only your own.

If you are an employee, start where you are. Identify the problems and issues you want to solve and begin formulating and pitching solutions. Negotiate room to innovate. Prove you can handle more responsibility, overcome more adversity, and solve more significant problems. And the world will give you more responsibility, more difficulty, and more prominent problems to solve.

If you are a manager, engage your team. Give them room and encourage them to innovate. Create space for them to test new ideas, and when those ideas don't work—and even if they do—celebrate the effort and the learnings, not the result. Your role is to help your team step into more personal responsibility.

And if you are an owner or member of the C-Suite, you have similar responsibilities as the manager above, and you are accountable for the outcomes as well. Your role is to help build new systems that encourage individuals to step into more responsibility. Moreover, you have to do it without undercutting your organization's current operations.

No one knows for certain what the future of work will look like, but we can see trends and apply principles that will help us adapt to change and more importantly, invent new ways of working. Reading and applying the information in this book is a great next step. Welcome to the journey!

HOW COMPANIES CREATE COSTS BY IGNORING EMPLOYEE WELL-BEING

by Dawna Jones, From Insight to Action

In a quest to be profitable and drive shareholder value at any cost, companies ignore one of the biggest influences on the bottom line: workplace emotional health. If people are not well, neither is the company.

Humans have an innate need to express creative talent. Suppressing that expression is the biological cause of depression and other stress-related illnesses. Understanding the deep human need for expression is fundamental to creating better workplaces responsive to change.

The opportunity lies in seeing the interrelationship between profit, purpose, and passion and a broader beneficial role for business in society. Then decisions can be informed, activating faster responses to changing conditions. Risk is not avoided but put to advantage. And the company is not unconsciously throwing money away or undermining its performance potential.

Traditional companies run on autopilot, like a self-driving car. Unlike a self-driving car, traditional companies are not using sensors their employees innately have to navigate effectively in complex conditions. Instead, ingrained fixed beliefs drive decisions, and a plethora of metrics focused on profit and shareholder value measure the results while employees suffer from aiming for uninspiring goals.

Even when companies talk about valuing people, decisions reveal an underlying belief that capital assets have a higher value. Underperforming workplaces—or at worse, toxic workplace relationships—are the result. Valuable creative talent is disengaged and reduced to barely coping. Decisions are limited to staying psychologically safe, given that trust is low. Human sensory capacity in the form of intuitive intelligence—essential for steering through complex and uncertain economic change—has been taken off-line by failure to pay attention to the health of workplace interrelationships. The value of diverse perspectives and sensitivities is muted by bias in decisions.

With an increased level of awareness, companies can do much better to be more human and far more adaptive.

In self-driving cars, different kinds and numbers of sensors conduct navigation: ultrasonic, image, radar, light detection and ranging sensors, and cloud sensors[11], which require costly rare earth minerals to operate. Combined, they must be better than a human to drive the car safely. They must pay attention to and quickly respond to changing conditions.

Similarly, combining diverse sensibilities unique to each human can provide better navigation for the individual, team, and company. Humans do not require rare earth minerals to function (of which a value of $70 billion are now found in landfills, thanks to linear thinking). However, the sensors in humans and, collectively, in companies, are

---

[11]   http://www.thedrive.com/tech/8657/
heres-how-the-sensors-in-autonomous-cars-work

underutilized and rarely acknowledged as holding strategic value to working in complex conditions.

Sensors in autonomous cars operate like bat sonar, pinging the surrounding environment to detect hard obstacles—things humans see naturally. Ship and plane navigation sensors substitute for human foresight. Cloud sensors mimic contextual awareness, and light and detection sensors fill in gaps to deeply perceive the hidden objects often in plain sight, at least intuitively.

Traditional companies today run with lagging indicators of performance that leave them looking backward in the rear view mirror rather than forward prepared for what lies ahead. While companies rely heavily on technology, they too often overlook the powerful natural human potential working for them; human potential repressed by being told what to do, suppressing the initiative needed for innovation and creativity.

Releasing creative talent will require injecting inspiration to pivot from a narrow profit-first decision-making focus to a broader focus tied to a significant purpose. Then the individual data points like key result areas, lagging and leading metrics, and other indicators can reveal overtly where and how energy is wasted and unethical decisions are being made, creating unnecessary costs and loss of reputation. Volkswagen's emission scandal is a perfect example of how executive direction created the conditions for unethical decision making through some creative algorithms by VW engineers.[12]

In a complex world, innate human sensors primed to detect changing conditions and to respond quickly will

---

12   https://ideas.darden.virginia.edu/2016/10/
      vw-emissions-and-the-3-factors-that-drive-ethical-breakdown/

determine how successful a company is at matching the rate of change.

The inherent leadership challenge involves reducing reliance on the technical and mechanical process tools to compel, direct, or incentivize performance. They can then emphasize workplace decision-making climates imbued with trust and open to receiving natural human potential and desire to collaborate. Then, companies can capitalize on the real opportunity to become too valuable to fail.

1. BLIND SIDE: COSTS CREATED BY IGNORING WORKPLACE HEALTH

STRESS-RELATED ILLNESS

Depression and anxiety are the leading causes of disability globally, according to the World Health Organization. The WHO counts an estimated 300 million human stories worldwide[13]–stories of undetected signals of depression, loss of value, and self-worth that, in some cases, lead to suicide. These include stories of careers destroyed and family life reduced to barely functional. These ailments cost the US economy $1 trillion each year. Dollar figures associated with workplace stress fail to open an empathic window to the loss of quality of life and wider social impact. When stress goes unrecognized, and stigma is applied, the workplace is a part of the problem. Even toxic workplaces become the "norm" after a period. Safe, supportive environments are essential.

Rarely discussed is another kind of stress. "Eustress" has a beneficial value to the individual's health and performance.

Knowing that some kinds of stress are beneficial and others not begs the question: What is the difference between the stress that depletes and destroys health and the stress

---

[13]   http://www.who.int/mediacentre/factsheets/fs369/en

that is of benefit? And is it true that stress is the fault of a lack of resilience skills at the individual level?

Unfortunately, in many workplaces, the prevailing belief is that if you are depressed, you are weak. The stigma is systemic, which compounds the time it takes for recovery. Attempting to label a complex condition creates the stigma by simplifying it. In a high- stress environment, individual and collective decision-making will be compromised. Averting the cost of poor decisions and compromised health requires taking a closer look at the biological dynamics.

Workplace stress-related illness is an indicator of company health.[14] It is not the consequence of an individual's capacity or inability to work in untenable conditions.

People do not want to become burnt out, depressed, or suffer from stress-related illness. That's not the idea when you wake up each morning. Each person goes to work wanting to contribute. But a breakdown in coping skills inevitably occurs when employees must meet metrics that do not matter, and they face pressure to churn out profit. Routine practices that simply do not fit the reality of market and business conditions burn out the very talent needed for company resilience.

Executives in traditional companies wouldn't want to admit it, but their employees are barely coping, in part, because the pressure of volatile global conditions is being off-loaded to employees. Instead of responding with awareness, the reaction is to work harder and faster—pushing people toward burnout because they care about their work. To stay healthy, keep pace, and remain relevant to society and customers, a company must restore heart and agility.

---

[14]   https://www.stress.org/stress-research

SPOTTING THE SIGNS OF BARELY COPING

An observant manager can see the signals that their work-place is under too much pressure.

It starts with the individual. The joy of getting up and going to work is gone.

You lose heart for your work. It is a real effort to show up. At the end of the day, you feel drained of energy.

It is hard to focus or meet deadlines. Important details are missed because the volume of information is overwhelming.

You are easily irritated by people and feel like running away from home or hiding in a dark cave.

The malaise spreads to the workplace:

Fear builds around the capacity to meet deadlines since not all members of the team are performing to potential.

Judgment from others immediately follows, fed by the belief that the environment you're in doesn't affect you. It does. People shoulder the blame and sink further. The rate of absenteeism goes up. Even those who come to work are not able to do their best. They are quickly assessed as non-performers and funneled into the performance management system, which fails to meet human needs in epic proportions.

Decision-making is compromised, and options narrow as the reduced level of vitality impacts the desire to accept risks and be creative. "Innovation" becomes a meaningless buzzword. Fear channels decisions into spin cycles sticking to the familiar.

If this sounds familiar, it is not too late to reverse the cause and save the human, financial and societal costs.

Increasingly, executives see workplace health from a more holistic perspective. Virgin Pulse[15] reports that well-being

---

[15]   http://community.virginpulse.
com/2017-business-of-healthy-employees

programs are top of mind and recognized as a top driver in engagement. Holding a broader perspective may allow the stigma of stress-induced illness to be replaced by a focus on workplace relationships, use of power and control, and other factors affecting expression (or, on the other hand, repression of talent).

Outside of the US, mental health has greater acceptance according to Virgin Pulse's academic team, Dr. Rajiv Kumar, Chief Medical Officer, and Dr. David Batman, Science Advisory Board, Virgin Pulse. In the US, extrinsic motivators like financial incentives work more effectively to engage employees in their well-being. In Europe, they point out that motivation is intrinsic; self-responsibility is higher, and self-reliance is greater. One could also expect that self-efficacy, the belief that a positive outcome is within your creative control, would be higher outside of the US as well.

The stigma of stress-related illness assumes the person lacks resilience. Ironically, it is the workplace that fails to be resilient. In the workplace, resilience is a community affair. The network of co-workers, when not struggling to survive the day, collectively provide the supportive safety net needed to gain strength and learn from each setback. In workplaces where the sense of belonging, support, and care is low, those who are not receiving the support they need wind up in the performance management system. Their worth as employees or partners capable of contributing value to the company is lost.

DOES YOUR WORKPLACE SUPPORT OR SUPPRESS SAFETY AND EXPRESSION?

The external environment is saturated with emotional data that gets interpreted as "safe" or "unsafe." Add the focus of your thinking, negative-positive or neutral, and your brain interprets the data to determine whether it is safe for you to be you and to express yourself in any given situation. Contributing to the sense of psychological and social safety is the unnoticed presence of unconscious bias. Bias is embedded in interpersonal communication and decisions like pay equity and actions. Combined, these streams of data accumulate as indirect messages about your value, your place in the world, and a sense of belonging, all of which are core to human health. That makes signals for depression subtle and cumulative as well as uniquely personal.

In her article *What I Wish I Knew*[16], Mandi Luis-Buckner reports symptoms like a sense of blurriness, guilt about letting your team down, irritability, tasks that feel emotionally overwhelming, or fear of losing your job or your income may mark the spot on the downward spiral where the heart's energy becomes increasingly depleted. Collective performance is seriously compromised when the heart isn't fully engaged. Business performance is compromised, too.

The external environment and workplace interpersonal communications, combined with management and communication style, directly set the safety for expression. Companies that manage themselves through statistics rather than collective accomplishment are guilty of creating unsafe workplaces that suppress the creative expression employees need for rapid response. Obviously, reversing that dynamic is not that complicated, but it does require thinking differently to restore a sense of humanity to the workplace environment. Metrics drive dynamics. How human are yours in your company?

---

[16]   http://www.mentalhealthworks.ca/what-i-wish-i-knew

RECOVERING WORKPLACE HEALTH; TRANSFORMING WORKPLACES

To move from using a command and directional stance to a peer-to-peer relationship, management needs a more sophisticated set of skills than is required by directing performance. If company executives are astute enough to recognize the bold role they must take in moving out of the rut and into a transformational process, workplace health can be recovered so that stress serves a positive benefit and value.

ATTRIBUTE #1: CARE

Business has a big impact on world resources and on the mental, emotional, and social health of communities, including the community inside the company getting the work done. Care is a core value that engages decision-making at the heart level. Without a full-hearted effort, the fuel companies rely on for performance is being siphoned off rather than aligned with purpose, meaning, and impact. True leadership doesn't come from logic. It comes from the heart. A clear heart, unencumbered by fear, anxiety, or the stress of not meeting commitments, makes foresight available. You can see what lies ahead, or at minimum, you feel confident that you can handle with ease whatever comes. Taking the time to center decisions at the heart level will support the most accurate decision. The intellect or mental faculty knows how to implement. The heart follows what has meaning and value.

ATTRIBUTE #2: AGILITY

Agility is a familiar word and probably overused, spanning everything from emotional to cognitive agility. Recovering workplace health requires both emotional and cognitive agility. Most companies rely on analytical thinking, which does not allow for a wide holistic perception. Broadening one's perspective is one way to move away from narrow aims to wider benefit. Companies tend to reward analytical thinking. Greater diversity is needed to solve the wicked problems business and society needs today. Although the desire is for creativity, if the environment values certainty, the messiness of creativity creates enough discomfort to attempt to control the creative process. The opportunity at the leadership level is to gain far more comfort with uncertainty, which naturally leads to growth.

Centralized decision-making is proving to be no match for the speed required, so many companies are advancing their agility through self-management at the team or organizational level or by distributing decision-making. Haier is an excellent example of the value of agility in transformation.[17] Rebuilt through self-managed teams, Haier, a Chinese company, has reinvented itself multiple times, growing from a company drowning in debt in 1984 to the world's largest home appliance manufacturer[18], with global revenues exceeding $32 billion in 2014 and profits of $2.4 billion.

Other companies that regularly reinvent themselves employ bio-mimicry management[19], a practice that enlists the life-affirming attributes of nature, including values-driven decision-making.

---

[17] http://www.huffingtonpost.com/entry/ haier-elevation_us_58b08fa0e4b02f3f81e446f8

[18] http://www.prnewswire.com/news-releases/ haier-tops-euromonitors-major-appliances-globa l-brand-rankings-for-seventh-consecutive-year-300206919.html

[19] http://www.huffingtonpost.com/great-work-cultures/ do-companies-that-mimic-n_b_12674962.html

2. Blind Side: Impaired Decision Making Caused by Bad Habits

You have seen it. So have I. Walk into a workplace or team environment and witness the go-go-go approach to getting things done. There is no time to reflect, think, or select the best approach to match the context and situation. Just run like mad. Underneath high speed, high pressure, and fast-paced workplace environments is an imbalance between reflection and action.

The terms masculine and feminine tend to be associated with gender, not a quality or state of being. Individuals and communities of people share the feminine and masculine essence: receptivity and action, respectively. Typically, conversation focuses on gender differences, which sometimes helps understanding and sometimes negatively reinforces territorial lines of identity. In actuality, the state of balance between feminine and masculine essence is inherent to each person and organization. Achieving balance is found by paying attention to the dance between receptivity: listening and sensing the environment, and action: making things happen with or without a clear vision or shared goal.

Imbalance also reveals the shadow side, observable in personal behavior and organizational dynamics. Danaan Parry, in his book *Warriors of the Heart,* states: "On the male journey to wholeness: Violence comes not from any innate masculine drive, but rather from the denial of the deepest levels of our masculinity."

He goes on to describe the shadow side of the imbalanced feminine:

"In recent years, we have tried to one degree or another to let go of macho male and manipulative female ways of expressing our needs... we are beginning to hear the soft wisdom of our inner voice, our intuitive self.... Our world cries out for men and women to move beyond their role-playing and their guilt and to unlock that deep, fertile naturalness that lives in us. Humankind hungers for good, grounded male energy, just as surely as it hungers for clear, deep, powerful woman energy. The integration of those creative forces will birth something very new, very wonderful."[20]

The point is to maintain and sustain balance: physically, between your feminine and masculine aspects, emotionally, and energetically through your relationship to your Self. When you lose touch with what you truly want from life, it will be because you are focused on being busy with not enough reflection. This can happen to anyone regardless of gender. It can also happen to organizations, companies included.

RESTORING BALANCE BETWEEN ACTION AND RECEPTIVITY

Over the next five years, technological innovation will challenge humanity to raise consciousness in response to the impact of artificial intelligence, robotics, distributed ledgers, and augmented reality/virtual reality in workplaces and homes. The change is not restricted to technology. Ecological life support systems on the planet have been taxed to the max – to the point where resilience has been depleted and breakdowns are occurring.

Bees, according to the USDA[21], provide 11 to 15 billion dollars annually worth of pollination services. Their extinction would remove ice cream from the shelves (and much more), and the price of food would go up, assuming

---

[20] *Warriors of the Heart* by Danaan Parry, published by BookSurge Publishing; 6th printing edition (Dec 16 2009) page 153

[21] https://www.ars.usda.gov/research/publications/publication/?seqNo115=311612

a technical means is found to pollinate food plants relying on bee pollination. U.S. naturalist E.O. Wilson asserts that if man disappeared, there would be a few disappointed armpit parasites, but if ants disappeared, the entire ecosystem would collapse.

The interrelationships are not observable until you take several steps back to look at the big picture and reflect on the patterns of decisions inside companies or to observe the effect of the wrong metrics on human behavior, motivation, or creativity. Going full tilt on automatic decision-making mode tempts organizations to dismiss anomalies to routine patterns, thereby eliminating insight – the portal for innovation and risk mitigation.[22] Nor can you benefit from the collective intuition that permits foresight needed to avoid being pushed to the wall through crisis.

To restore balance between full-on 24/7 action and be able to anticipate or foresee the impact of any one of the "disruptors" seemingly emerging out of nowhere:

Take reflection walks with the entire team, preferably in nature. The aim is to gather observations on what the organization repeatedly does that effectively blocks creative contribution or wastes money. The way to do it is to not focus, allowing observations to show up from the subconscious. If companies can unknowingly toss $70 billion worth of rare earth minerals in landfills, what kind of decisions would save that money and those resources? What other resources are being thrown out that could be repurposed or resold?

Slow your mind down to be present with yourself and others. Take mindfulness training. Reclaim control over

---

[22] Listen to Gary Klein explain the value of insights on an episode 30 of the Insight to Action podcast https://shows.pippa.io/insight-to-action-inspirational-insights-podcast

your focus. Then you can reclaim control over what the company is focused on.

Listen to the outlier voices conveying a message that you do not want to hear but need to. Companies that have failed have received the signals long beforehand, but either ignored them or chose to ignore them. Kodak is the poster child for seeing the future and then pretending not to notice when it invented the digital camera and then stuck to its existing business model rather than embracing change. Risk-taking is a required part of leadership, not to be avoided or rationalized into submission.

Book downtime for the entire team or business unit. Play and play. Do not focus on any problems. Then, sit down and collate your observations. Sometimes the best way to see the obvious is to detach so you can better see the interactions from a wider perspective.

The cost of acting without reflecting results in failure to learn from big mistakes or flawed assumptions. The idea is not to be error free but to know why things went wrong so you can strengthen your decision-making muscle and gain clarity. What is the cost of some of the worst decisions your company has made? Direct? Indirect? Identify those costs, human and financial, and you will find a reason to learn and a way to save costs.

3. BLIND SIDE: FROM DISENGAGED EMPLOYEES TO HIGH-PERFORMANCE NETWORKS

Work must have meaning and a positive impact to be engaging. Across generations, people seek to contribute and make a positive impact. Today's world is confusing and disheartening for some. For others, it is a palette to design a better world. Past business practices have regularly ignored the impact of decisions on employee and workplace health; and community, society and ecological health. When statistics like the high cost of disengaged employees are tossed about as a problem to solve, it signals something profoundly wrong in how workplaces are designed and cared for. The Engagement Institute estimates the costs of disengagement at $450-550 billion dollars per year. Not trivial. Again, those costs are higher when you take into account the waste of human talent, the indirect cost of poor decisions, and failure to engage human potential. Companies are working on changing this figure and can do so faster with bold decisions and conscious, caring leadership.

The highest leverage point is through providing an environment where people can take their full spectrum of intelligence to work. Peter Senge, in 1999, called it "spiritual intelligence": the space, freedom, and safety to bring our whole Selves to work.

"Spirit at work involves profound feelings of well-being, a belief that one's work makes a contribution, a sense of connection to others and common purpose, an awareness of a connection to something larger than self, and a sense of perfection and transcendence."[23]

The manager's role is shifting from controlling and directing employees to supporting their creative contribution and to creating the environment, a sense of connection. He or she cannot do it in isolation or alone.

Anne Murray Allen, when she was at Hewlett Packard, conducted research to discover what was at the source of consistently phenomenal performance. In an "Evolutionary Provocateur" podcast[24], we discussed the qualities of high-performance networks.

---

[23]   KaizenSolutions.org/paths.pdf

[24]   https://itunes.apple.com/au/artist/dawna-jones/id1218439755?mt=2

"We learned that the high-performance networks of collaboration were ones where people were seen by each other as legitimate contributors. In those high performing networks, people had a palpable sense of social well-being. They felt loved and cared for by their co-workers; love in the sense that they were seen as legitimate contributors. They weren't invisible. They were listened to. They knew that what they said mattered and that people truly cared about them as individuals. If something was wrong or affecting them negatively, their network cared about them and would often make movements to support them or pick up the slack to support coworkers while meeting the mission at hand."[25]

Workplaces that work for people are grounded in a strong sense of purpose to serve a goal much greater than any one person. Companies that deliberately pay attention and design organizations for people recognize profit is the result of a valuable contribution. It is not the purpose of a company.

Traditional capitalists see profit as the purpose, viewing it as heresy to state otherwise. Those days are over. Countless companies who operate from genuine care demonstrate otherwise. From Vulcan Tech to Virgin to companies that mimic life[26], profitability far exceeds anything companies known for unethical behavior and profit or shareholder value focused. Though their numbers are few, they are growing. Purpose is not narrow and aimed at benefiting the few. It is inspirational and benefits employees, the communities they serve, and the ecological systems.

---

[25] Podcast interview with Anne Murray Allen on the Evolutionary Provocateur podcast, iTunes EP62 February, 2010

[26] *Companies That Mimic Life* by Joseph Bragdon outlines seven exemplar companies where the cultural DNA is organized around the principles of life.

The purpose of companies today must be to restore care for the impact economic activities have on economic, social and ecological health not to do less harm but to regenerate and restore. The inconvenient truth is that unless business takes a higher road, shifting from a narrow point of view to a global and caring worldview, the widening disconnection between man and Nature will grow, and humanity will fail.

Neil deGrasse Tyson ✓
@neiltyson

Follow

Odd that our measures of animal intelligence are often tests of what humans do best rather than of what they do best.

11:23 AM - 16 Sep 2016

The real test of intelligence is to recognize changing conditions and then to rise above the conflict created and the adversity and to expand our intelligence. While we pride ourselves as the most intelligent species, unhealthy workplaces reveal failure to learn and adapt. Growth is required for all to attain a higher level of conscious awareness and leadership and to access the advanced decision-making skills that use human strengths while compensating for cognitive bias. Be bold.

FROM PROFIT TO PURPOSE: HOW PURPOSE-DRIVEN LEADERSHIP DRIVES COMPANIES TO THRIVE (AND STILL MAKE MONEY)

by Ozlem Brooke Erol, Purposeful Business

A great company is one that spreads joy and fulfillment and makes the world a better place because it exists, not simply a company that outperforms the market with a certain percentage over a certain period of time.
- Firms of Endearment

If we talked a decade ago about creating businesses with a *clear purpose* that is deep and *meaningful to employees and clients*, there would have been a lot more resistance embracing this concept. The biggest goal has always been about maximizing profit and the biggest concern to making shareholders happy. "When you are responsible to shareholders to generate the highest profit, you cannot put a lot of focus on purpose for employers or clients. That does not work. It is unrealistic," many say to this day.

Unfortunately, the biggest barrier to creating purpose in business has been the short-term shareholder pressure that hinders management's ability to focus on long-term value creation.

The good news is that we are talking more about purpose. Oxford University and Ernst and Young (EY) found that public dialog on purpose has increased fivefold between 1995 and 2016.)[27] And amazing organizations are having stellar results by integrating purpose into their business strategy.

WHAT DOES "PURPOSE" MEAN FOR BUSINESS?

Let's start with the meaning of the word "purpose." The one I love the most is from EY[28] "a human-centered, socially-engaged conception that seeks to create value for a broad set of stakeholders." So it is not only to please a group of stakeholders but all of them: clients, employees, shareholders, vendors, suppliers, community. It is an aspirational reason for being that is grounded in humanity.[29] No group gains at the expense of other stakeholder groups; they all prosper together, says the book *Firms of Endearment*.[30]

---

[27] State of the debate on purpose in business EY Beacon Institute (https://www.ey.com/Publication/vwLUAssets/ ey-the-state-of-the-debate-on-purpose-in-business/%24FILE/ ey-the-state-of-the-debate-on-purpose-in-business.pdf)

[28] EY website (https://www.ey.com/Publication/vwLUAssets/ ey-the-state-of-the-debate-on-purpose-in-business/%24FILE/ ey-the-state-of-the-debate-on-purpose-in-business.pdf)

[29] Great reasons in http:www.ey.com/Publication/vwLUAssets/ ey-the-state-of-the-debate-on-purpose-in-business/$FILE/ ey-the-state-of-the-debate-on-purpose-in-business.pdf

[30] *Firms of Endearment*, Foreword XXIII

The International Institute for Management Development (IMD)[31] echoes these ideas, defining purpose as "a company's core 'reason for being.' The organization's single underlying objective that unifies all stakeholders and embodies its ultimate role in the broader economic, societal and environmental context."

Purpose can be said to inform the mission, vision, and values of a company, but it has a wider scope.[32] It is less about which products or services your company offers and more about why and how.

A definite purpose is contagious. It clarifies to people what to expect from the company, but also what to expect from each other. It is inclusive and resonates with people from all levels within the company, without restrictions as to the understanding and motivational value of it in place or time.[33]

At an individual level, finding and living your purpose is the highest form of fulfillment, which is more lasting than happiness. Studies now show there are three tiers of happiness:

1) Pleasure - chasing next high; hard to maintain

2) Passion - flow; peak performance; time flies by

3) Higher purpose - being part of something bigger than yourself.[34]

---

[31] https:www.imd.org

[32] https://www.ey.com/Publication/vwLUAssets/ey-the-state-of-the-debate-on-purpose-in-business/%24FILE/ey-the-state-of-the-debate-on-purpose-in-business.pdf

[33] http://switchandshift.com/7-provoking-questions-critical-to-your-purpose-in-business

[34] *Delivering Happiness: A Path to Profits, Passion, and Purpose* by Tony Hsieh

Is purpose new? No, but the purpose-led transformation is.[35] It is far more like a revelation, a rediscovery of what the business set out to do originally.

WHAT BROUGHT US HERE?

Why do we talk and read more about purpose now? What changed during the last decades? Why is this a more important topic than before? What made it more acceptable to talk and believe it—when the objections were pretty solid?

The system that worked to maximize profit at all cost—the way we did it for 150-plus years (from the industrial age and beyond)—does not work anymore. What we did as leaders of organizations twenty years ago does not seem to give us the same results. There are a lot of new variables in place, discussed throughout this book, which do not create the outcomes we expect. Most organizations feel out of sync with what is happening; many do not recognize what the real issue is either. It is a time to be proactive to thrive, but the path is not necessarily so clear when changes hit organizations at a very fast pace.

WHAT DOES NOT WORK ANYMORE?

Command/control: "When I tell my employees what to do and how to do it, I get a lot of resistance. They want to make their own decisions."

Salary/pay being the biggest motivator for employees: "I even give them more money, and they still leave the company." (Daniel Pink tells so eloquently how carrots and

---

sticks don't work in his book *Drive* and names it Motivation 2.0.[36])

Hierarchical organizational structure: "We have layers of good people to trickle down the messages and manage people, but this structure does not seem to work anymore. The silos of different departments tend to drive people apart, and nothing gets done. There is no efficient collaboration among the departments."

Promotion based on tenure: "We promote people who have given many years of their lives to work here, but new people who bring better results are upset."

Once-a-year performance reviews: "We have an intense two-hour review where the managers tell their team members how they are doing. People do not want to wait for a year now for feedback."

Job description and roles: "Everybody has an unambiguous job description, so they know exactly what to do and what they are responsible for. Employees want to be involved in areas that are not part of their roles. If they do anything and everything, it will be chaos, right?"

And the biggest—a job is a means to an end: "This is a job, you are not supposed to love it, you are lucky to have this job; just work hard and be here from at least 8 a.m. to 6 p.m. every day." (This one certainly does not work anymore. Chuck Blakeman talks about these industrial-age mindset diseases in his book *Why Employees Are Always a Bad Idea*.[37])

---

[36] *Drive* by Daniel Pink, page 32
[37] *Why Employees Are Always a Bad Idea* by Chuck Blakeman talks about the industrial age diseases

BUT WHY ALL THIS CHANGE?

First of all, as *Reinventing Organizations* by Frederic Laloux[38] puts it, organizations and humans went through several stages of consciousness to get here (from infrared to teal organizations). Organizational history shows changes reflected prevailing worldview and consciousness. Every time there was an increase in consciousness, how we formed and led organizations changed.

We bought into the industrial age mindset—which still exists in the front offices of many organizations—as *Reinventing Organizations* would define as Orange. This mindset told us to believe outdated practices (like command/control, hierarchical organizational structures, etc.) were the best ways of doing business and paved the road for success. Those principles worked (at least in some aspects) for a while, maybe for a few generations. People were happy to work hard to make a living, and work was not supposed to bring meaning or be aligned with who you are. Success was measured solely by titles, promotions, how long you stayed with a company, and how much money you make. The belief at the time was employees, for the most part, were lazy, not dependable, and not intelligent enough[39] (based on Frederick Taylor's principles of scientific management).

Shareholder value was the biggest priority of these orange organizations. Profit was the dominating story. It certainly was not all bad; there were many successful organizations in this era. Some of the impact it had on workers, their families, and their well-being was not measured, though. These rules of business demanded a high price for success.

And, as Laloux defines so amazingly in *Reinventing Organizations*, as the consciousness level increased,

---

[38] *Reinventing Organizations* by Frederic Laloux
[39] *Reinventing Organizations* by Frederic Laloux, page 109

value-based organizations that care about purpose emerged—the "Green" organizations.[40] Leaders are in service to those whom they lead. The latest evolution of organization is "Teal," where leaders get rid of their egos and find out more about themselves. They form companies or lead organizations knowing their purpose in life.

With these changes and other factors, employees' and clients' expectations have changed drastically. We are more conscious of whom we buy from, how we use our money, where we invest, and how we work. Our values have shifted for the betterment of humanity and an awareness of our connection to each other. Now as consumers, we want to know how companies treat their employees and how they manufacture their products (environmental protection, social responsibility) before we buy from them. We are more aware of the damage we do to our planet. We recognize how and what we do as individuals and organizations have an impact on our future. As our overall education and awareness increase, concern about the common issues of humanity increases as well.

Aspiration-reality gap

In our media-savvy world, the public is quick to spot any distance between what a company is and what it says it is. Big corporations often advertise—especially on the Sunday morning news shows—how well they treat their employees and how much they prioritize client service. It does not matter what they say; as employees and customers, we know if what organizations say reflects the truth about them or not. We care about corporate trust and integrity. Consumers and stakeholders do not trust some brands. As

---

[40]   *Reinventing Organizations*: Green Organizations

the information flow is democratized, we as consumers can follow the truth.

The tyranny of organizations

As members of Generation X (born between 1965 to 1981) entered the workforce, the formula and the system that worked for years started to collapse. Why? In addition to the many factors Laloux mentions, organizations began to get rid of their people in big numbers when the times were tough. Employees felt they had no guarantee of stability, even if they worked hard. (And Millennials, their children, were watching.) They saw their colleagues—people who had attended the best schools, worked hard, earned great grades, and who had amazing jobs—were still getting laid off. So Gen X started questioning if it was worth it to be so loyal and tolerate the environments in which they worked just for money. They started asking what mattered most in life and wanted to make sure they made time for family. (By the way, generations before them have always said that family came first, too, but they could not reflect it in their daily lives. Organizations did not let their people be flexible. In fact, work always had to come first.) Gen Xers found it very conflicting to work in environments in which they had to separate their work and personal life. Even if they tried, it did not work. It was the first time women were at work in greater numbers. (Women make up 47 percent of the workforce now.[41]) There were more missed school plays and ballgames because both parents worked at organizations that allowed very little time for family.

---

[41] https://blog.dol.gov/2017/03/0
1/12-stats-about-working-women

35

Different (and common) generational values

Questioning the status quo became more common as Millennials joined the workforce. They certainly did not want to sacrifice time with their families, as their parents or grandparents did. They did not see rewards in living like that. They saw hard-working people struggling with their finances, losing their homes, and accumulating debt. They found no guarantee that working for someone else would assure job security. As they get closer to retirement, baby boomers started asking the same questions as Millennials do: "What matters most, and how can I be myself at work and everywhere else? How can I add more meaning to my everyday life, which should include my job? I spend most of my time at work." So these big questions became a common conversation.

Can we blame anyone for wanting more meaning in their lives and choosing to enjoy every day instead of only chasing the weekends? That does not mean we can slack off. We all have to bring results. We all have the reality we share: we still need to make a living. But at least now it is tilted toward bringing more meaning into our lives as individuals and organizations. Greg Easterbrook says, "A transition from material want to meaning want is in progress on a historically unprecedented scale—involving hundreds of millions of people—may eventually be recognized as the principal cultural development of our age."[42]

Change of mindset

Adults who can make good decisions everywhere else every day can be trusted to make the best decisions at work. They do not need to be told what to do. If we stop treating adults

---

[42] *The Progress Paradox* by Gregg Easterbrook, page 317

like children, they take more responsibility, they get more creative, and they bring better results. The fixed mindset of some old-school-thinking leaders has to change. We must embrace a growth mindset, which shows nothing is static, and there is always room for improvement. Carol Dweck researches motivation and growth mindset—the idea that we can grow our brain's capacity to learn and to solve problems. "In a school in Chicago, if a student didn't get a passing grade, they got the grade *not yet*," Dweck shares in an informative and inspiring TED talk. "If you get the grade "*not yet*," you understand you are on a learning curve. It gives you a path to the future."[43]

Technology/ IQ/EQ

Rapid changes in technology are impacting how we work. Most of us don't need to be at a corporate office anymore because our computers are at our fingertips. Automation, AI, and robotics are assuming jobs that require some left brain skills or repetitive, mundane tasks. Emotions have existed in the business world like the elephant in the room for a long time, and now we acknowledge it. In this new environment, some of the right-brain skills like emotional intelligence (EQ) that makes us human are getting more attention. How can we integrate more EQ in our lives? We valued employees with high IQs for a long time, for good reasons, and paid them better. What about people with soft skills like compassion, empathy, altruism, self-awareness, and communication? What if we value both IQ and EQ equally? Might we begin to not only create technology but also see the implications of technology on our humanity?

---

[43]   Carol Dweck, TED talk: https://www.ted.com/talks/ carol_dweck_the_power_of_believing_that_you_can_improve

Emotionally intelligent companies value emotions and right-brain skills woven throughout their culture.[44]

Hiring

Traditional hiring processes are becoming obsolete. Online job search systems require applicants to upload a resume and then enter the information—all which may be found on the resume—into searchable fields. Too often candidates are asked why they want a particular job and why they will be a better fit than anyone else. Who can answer such a question? We are moving away from these old practices because they do not serve organizations nor the applicants. Organizations cannot find the best match; candidates lose a lot of good opportunities without the best tools to reach the right positions where they can excel. We also have a lot more jobs in a lifetime now and gain different skill sets, making the ads that look for "ten-plus years of experience in the same field or job title" obsolete as well.

Our passion and purpose become differentiators now as we apply to jobs or start new businesses. If we are excited about what we do, people feel that enthusiasm. Clients and employees care about this passion now. Leaders who can see how the future will unfold prefer people who are aligned with the company values and purpose above their expertise. Today's leaders are innovating the hiring process and may not even require resumes. They want employees who are a good fit with the culture, who are passionate about the work, and who resonate with the company purpose.

"The first thing we look for when hiring new staff is personality," says Richard Branson. "In my eyes, personality always wins over book smarts. Company knowledge

---

[44]   *Emotional Intelligence by* Daniel Goleman

and job-specific skills can be learned, but you can't train a personality."[45]

Crushing millions of souls

A recent Gallup poll found that disengagement in the American workplace has reached an astounding 70 percent. Humans eventually reach a threshold. The collective soul-crushing at work that began over 150 years ago is reaching its peak. Too many people lose their enthusiasm, passion, and spirit at work. Their ideas do not matter, they do not feel heard, they endure boring, repetitive work, they don't understand how what they do every day contributes to the company vision. No matter how much they work, they know they can be laid off. They feel they are not a good match, they work too many hours to keep their jobs, they miss many important family events, and so on. We experience together even if we have not experienced it individually; we see, we watch, we hear it all around us. Even if it is not conscious, we are feeling the heaviness together. We are at the breaking point of this human suffering required to earn a paycheck. When engagement rates are this low, too much potential is wasted.[46]

Advances in psychology

Advances in psychology and neuroscience keep us informed about what makes us human, how we function, and how we make decisions, which contributes to our new vision of

---

[45] Sir Richard Branson, Virgin Group Founder, "Purpose transformation" keynote address, Purpose Power: Driving Innovation and Growth, EY-sponsored event, 22 January 2015.

[46] http://www.gallup.com/poll/180404/ gallup-daily-employee-engagement.aspx

organizations. It is important to stay abreast of emerging research. Organizations consist of human beings after all.

Increasing lifespans

As we live longer, more vibrant lives, the fact is that that we may need—and want—to work longer. We all have an inner drive to do something meaningful. Maybe we can deal with a job that we don't like for twenty years, but what about forty or fifty years? At some point, we suffer emotionally or physically for doing something that does not mean anything but merely provides money.

HOW DO THESE CHANGES IMPACT ORGANIZATIONS?

An organization will not survive—much less thrive—with the old industrial mindset. Leaders must bring greater awareness of these changes—at the very least. Proactive leaders with a growth mindset will position their organizations to thrive in these times of drastic change in how we work.

The simplest and most significant awareness is that people are the most valuable asset an organization has. This isn't news, of course. The impact comes when an organization genuinely embodies this value every single day in the workplace. Everybody who interacts with an organization—who walks through the halls, who buys from it, or does business with it—can sense this commitment. It is not a value or mission statement written on a wall. If people are happy, the clients, the vendors, and the suppliers are happy, too. Happiness at work increases productivity, engagement, and tenure, and these translate into profit.

Leaders who understand these principles believe people can find meaning at work and that there is a big benefit when an employee knows how their daily work contributes to the company's goal, mission, and purpose. They know when employees do what they love and find meaning in what they do: they will be more engaged and more productive at work, versus looking forward to the end of the day. As an employer, whom would you want to recruit? One who is passionate about what they will do or the one who will work only for making money?

WHAT CAN LEADERS DO NOW?

Leaders who understand the dynamics of the world we live in and who are willing to do the work on themselves stay resilient in these changing times and know the biggest factor for their success lies in the hands of their people.

Create a clear definition of the purpose and communicate it

Too many people at all levels of organizations do not know why the company they work for exists. When asked, their best reply is: We are here to produce this product or offer this service. These organizations are focused on assuring maximum profit for the owner or shareholders and to sell the business one day. This way of operating is based on fear: fear of competition, fear of scarcity, fear of not being successful.

New "teal" companies do not concentrate on competition and scarcity but on innovation. They want to hear new ideas, and they encourage inspired contributions from their people. They come from an anticipation of abundance, not a fear of scarcity. They do not focus solely on taking the biggest portion of the market but to be the best in what they do. That is how they excel. They do not spend their valuable energy and resources on how to beat the competition but on how to be proactive in the new world we live in and stay innovative.

First, leaders must clearly define the purpose of the organization besides making a profit. They need to get feedback and insight from many stakeholders to do that. Then they must communicate it to their people, hire those people who get excited about the same purpose, show how each one contributes to this common purpose, create teams in which each member feels they belong, and treat every one of them with dignity and respect. When you create such an environment and are open to listening to new ideas, your people will bring their whole selves to work and do their best. You don't need to worry about the rest; your turnover, your engagement rates, and your numbers will reflect the positive results.

A strong and distinguishing purpose demonstrates a brand's unique contribution and the value it adds to the world, leaving a sense of emptiness should the brand disappear. Consumers relate to organizations that represent their values well. People want to work for these companies, and they want to buy from them. Vendors want to work with them, and suppliers want to do business with them. At the end, all stakeholders are happy.

Make purpose the biggest driver of business strategy

Coming up with an authentic purpose statement and communicating it effectively is crucial, but it is not enough. Creating a "purposeful business" means the purpose is not only spoken; it is integrated into business strategy. The purpose shines the guiding light when leaders make decisions. They ask, "Does this align with our purpose?"

Do the inner work as leaders

It requires a certain type of leader—and courage—to leave long-held disciplines and beliefs to step into the uncertain, the unknown.

Leaders who embrace the "teal" mindset create organizations that support people's longing to be themselves at work. They eliminate some ego-driven decisions that do not contribute to the overall success of the organization. They experience breakthroughs that encompass self-management, wholeness, and evolutionary purpose.[47] (Doug Kirkpatrick talks more about self-management in another chapter.) They bypass the norms about job definitions to create evolving roles in which people can pick up their responsibilities as they go, based on their talents and interests.

As in anything else, any change starts within us. If leaders, owners, and founders are not willing to do their inner work, check their egos, and discover what matters to them, they will find it hard to embrace these changes. The level of an organization's consciousness cannot exceed its leaders' consciousness levels. They need to strengthen qualities like vulnerability, trust, humility, authenticity, and courage.

These new mindset leaders and their organizations will not only enjoy the amazing results, but most importantly they will have the emotional satisfaction of doing the right thing for everyone and leaving a legacy that will enable the organization to thrive after they are gone. Even though we may not be consciously aware of it, we all have a longing to contribute to others. A good purpose speaks to your heart, not only your mind, and we are all emotional beings.

---

[47] "How teal organizations bring self-management." *Reinventing Organizations*, page 56

Fulfilling a universal need

This is nothing but going back to being a real human being who is innately programmed to make a difference in the world. What better way to do it as leaders who can impact stakeholders, their families, communities, and the world by doing what is right? It is not only a way to do business but a choice that will carry us all forward.

Today's leaders look at purpose as an important strategic tool. They realize a strong purpose can help an organization develop the capabilities and resilience necessary for continuous growth and transformation. The purpose-driven company is a humanistic organization that cares about all people, the community, and the world, and that contributes to the whole ecosystem.

AMAZING FINDINGS AND RESULTS ABOUT PURPOSE IN THE WORKPLACE:

Findings show that 87 percent believe[48] companies perform best over time if their purpose goes beyond profit, and 52 percent of companies are embracing the broad definition of purpose.

Executives identified several special ways in which embedding the pursuit of purpose in all that they do creates value:

- Building greater customer loyalty (52%)

- Followed by preserving brand value and reputation (51%)

---

[48]   https://www.ey.com/Publication/vwLUAssets/
EY-purpose-led-organizations/$FILE/
EY-purpose-led-organizations.pdf

- Attracting and retaining top talent (42%)

- Developing innovative new products and services (40%)

Purpose also matters for job satisfaction: 59 percent say it is very important and 37 percent say it is important. Only 1 percent say it is not important at all.

The 585 organizations who prioritized purpose are seeing 10-plus percent growth in their business in the last three years.

Benefits of purpose in business can be summed up in five easy ways:[49]

- Purpose instills strategic clarity

- Purpose channels innovation

- Purpose is a force for and a response to transformation

- Purpose taps a universal need

- Purpose builds bridges

- Some examples of successful purpose-driven companies:

Southwest Airlines has experienced thirty-three years of unbroken profitability when many airlines suffered in the last decades. They have a great vision and purpose. Their CEO Gary Kelly says, "Our people are our single greatest strength and most enduring long-term competitive advantage. Southwest Airlines's number one priority is to

---

[49]   https://www.ey.com/Publication/vwLUAssets/
ey-the-state-of-the-debate-on-purpose-in-business/%24FILE/
ey-the-state-of-the-debate-on-purpose-in-business.pdf

ensure the personal safety of each Southwest customer and employee. Beyond this, we follow 'The Golden Rule,' meaning that we treat each other the way we want to be treated, which is why doing the right thing by our employees and customers is so inherent to who we are as a company. We believe in Living the Southwest Way, which is to have a Warrior Spirit, a Servant's Heart, and a Fun-LUVing Attitude. Within each of these categories are specific behaviors to help us be a safe, profitable, and fun place to work."

It seemed odd to many when Whole Foods came up with a higher purpose to fulfill: creating value for all stakeholders.[50] Their purpose statement says: "With great courage, integrity, and love – we embrace our responsibility to co-create a world where each of us, our communities, and our planet can flourish. All the while, celebrating the sheer love and joy of food."

Konosuke Matsushita, founder of a Japanese electronics company, stated their purpose as "overcome poverty, to relieve society as a whole from misery, and bring it wealth." Note that this purpose has nothing to do with the products they manufacture.

Seventh Generation walks the talk of its purpose—and its employees and customers notice. The company encourages consumers to line-dry clothes[51] instead of machine drying, at the risk of cannibalizing its dryer sheet product. They are using their business to start a movement that will change an industry. This authenticity, potentially at the expense of their bottom line, inspires loyalty that no lip service will create. Their purpose says: "We are always evaluating how to reduce environmental impact, increase performance and safety, and create a more sustainable supply

---

[50]   *Firms of Endearment* Sisodia, Wolfe, Sheth, Foreword XV
[51]   https://www.seventhgeneration.com

chain. We believe it is our responsibility to set a course for a more mindful way of doing business, where companies act as partners with other stakeholders to create a brighter future for the whole planet."

Patagonia makes extremely durable outwear. When clothing lasts longer, consumers buy less frequently, which, of course, threatens to reduce sales. But Patagonia claims a higher mission and purpose: "Build the best product, cause no unnecessary harm, use business to inspire and implement solutions to the environmental crisis. For us at Patagonia, a love of wild and beautiful places demands participation in the fight to save them, and to help reverse the steep decline in the overall environmental health of our planet."

These beautiful and inspiring purposes go beyond making a profit, and these companies live it and mean it! We can all get inspired to do the same as leaders.

RELATIONSHIPS AND RITUALS: HOW TO KEEP COMPANY CULTURE FROM GOING WRONG IN TIMES OF RAPID GROWTH

by Josh Levine, Great Mondays

From sex in stairwells and absentee management to outright racism: a spate of news recently has covered cultures going awry in Silicon Valley. While the extreme cases on the left coast make headlines, errant cultures affect companies of all kind and size. Keeping culture from unraveling is a significant challenge every growth organization must learn to manage if its leaders intend to succeed in the long run.

In modest-sized organizations, a few individuals rely on one another to get work done, usually becoming a tight-knit bunch in the process. Let's call this an intimate community: *a group of people where "most of the members recognize and are recognized by many of the others."* By nature and necessity, when put together, individuals develop relationships, and when intimate communities form, they collective hold the "knowing"—the "who's" and "what's" of the organization.

(Everyone knows Shelby is the code base wizard; Sanjay said we broke our sales records last quarter.)

The connections in these communities enable this widespread knowing—where one person can have a sense of what's happening throughout the company. In turn, this knowing strengthens our connections. It's a self-reinforcing loop, where relationships serve as the synapses of business.

But what happens when hiring kicks into overdrive and more people show up for work? The number of relationships we need to manage explodes. At some point, it's too much for our brains, even with the help of new hire emails and org charts.

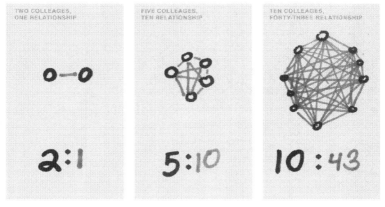

The number of relationships within an organization grows exponentially as each new colleague joins.

Constant growth, whether by acquisition or placement, diminishes the percentage of "who's" and "what's" each knows, eventually weakening the relationship of any one individual to the company as a whole. We tend to trust those with whom we have history. We understand their motivations and can predict how they'll react. What do we do when we find ourselves surrounded by people we don't quite recognize?

Relationships foster culture, but when those relationships become unmanageable, humans look to the safety of those they know and trust. Whether they realize it or not, every leader of every growth organization will face the phenomena of staff subdividing into intimate communities.

Leaders who want to *design* their culture, not just let it happen to them, ask: When does this subdivision begin? Does a magic number of employees compel culture changes? And what can be done about it?

If you've worked with another human, you know good relationships foster good work. These bonds are the conduits of culture, and while they don't guarantee success, you can be sure it ain't happening without them. Think of relationships as connective tissue: take this essential layer away, and business would just be a pile of old laptops and financial documents.

No blue-chip CEO will argue the point: the human side of business is critical to success. But how does this system of relationships change as startups emerge from their proverbial garages with dreams of long-term success? I propose an answer: relationship decay. As co-workers increase in number, our brains have to work harder to remember all the names, faces, and details. We are forced to choose who we know and how well.

Why should anyone care? Relationship decay is the reason startup cultures fail.

50

Without foresight and guidance, startup cultures weaken with growth. The deterioration is hardly noticeable at first, but when it gains momentum, employees will look around and no longer know all of the "who's" and "what's" that have contributed to the organization's cohesion. This is it: the moment culture is at its highest risk of unraveling. If we can see it coming, maybe we can prepare for it.

DR. DUNBAR, I PRESUME?

In 1993, British anthropologist Robin Dunbar theorized that as a group grows in size, it requires more relationship-strengthening activities or "social grooming" to operate effectively. In his research of primates, he observed that the more individuals in a group, the more relationships existed. The more relationships there are, the more social grooming is needed. The more social grooming that's needed, the more energy is required to maintain the group's structure. In fact, Dunbar observed that in nonhuman primates social grooming time is linearly related to group size.

How do they do it? It turns out for primates, social grooming is mainly achieved through actual grooming, but for humans it's language.

Maintaining stability of human-sized groups by grooming alone would make intolerable time demands. [...] the evolution of large groups in the human lineage depended on developing a more efficient method for time-sharing the processes of social bonding.

In human conversations, about 60 percent of time is spent gossiping about relationships and personal experiences. Language may accordingly have evolved to allow individuals to learn about the behavioral characteristics of other group members more rapidly than was feasible by direct observation alone.

Fascinating. But no matter how chatty we may be, even homo sapiens have an upper limit when it comes to group size. Dunbar concludes that groups can only grow so large—eventually what it takes to maintain the relationships outweighs the benefit of being together. When the number of individuals grows beyond 150, now known as Dunbar's Number, the group will divide or create subgroups. (Even author Malcolm Gladwell name-checked this phenomenon in his book *The Tipping Point*.)

Neighborhoods within towns, teams within leagues, and even clans within online communities are all examples of organized groups that more or less adhere to Dunbar's theory. So that's the moment of risk, yes? I wasn't so sure.

I had seen organizational culture go through significant change well before that. So I did some more digging. It turns out, when it comes to work, the wheels on the culture wagon may get wobbly way sooner than Dunbar might expect.

WHEN CULTURES GO COCKEYE

Internet cryptography pioneer Christopher Allen has tussled with Dunbar's number in a few well-written articles. In them he argues that groups subdivide at significantly less than 150—probably around fifty, he argues. Why? For groups that come together for reasons less demanding than true survival, the amount of energy required to maintain relationships above fifty individuals is greater than the benefit received. While corporate America's competitive environments can evoke "kill-or-be-killed" attitudes, we aren't fighting off large toothy predators like our hairier ancestors, even if sometimes it feels like it.

Add the layers of management, departments, and new locations that happen around this time and—*boom!*—culture spaghetti all over the floor.

Does Allen prove an exact number for this phenomenon? No. But it doesn't matter. When an organization subdivides and relationships weaken (or don't form in the first place), the story is the same nearly every time. Somewhere between fifty and 150, whether by talent acquisition or company acquisition, if strong relationships aren't fostered, culture is more than likely to go off the rails. And if leaders aren't looking, when they are finally forced to tangle with the symptoms of an unraveling culture, it may be too late.

The sooner founders and leaders realize that culture can and should be designed, the sooner they can think about how to strengthen relationships even as their organization grows beyond fifty, five hundred, or five thousand.

THE IMPORTANCE OF RITUALS

Now that we know that relationships begin to weaken somewhere between fifty and 150 people, how should leaders of growth organizations keep colleagues more tightly connected through bouts of early growth? Rituals. A ritual is a recurring group activity designed to strengthen relationships. People organize them among friends (poker night) and family (Thanksgiving dinner) because it gives us an opportunity to connect and share. And it feels good. The result of these get-togethers is a stronger bond, and companies have an opportunity to foster purposeful connections through rituals to counteract the relationship challenges of rapid growth.

Leadership can experience relationship decay as well. It isn't as obvious because they are surrounded by a purposefully small group of executives and possibly lead a small team. All the same, they lose touch with the "who's" and the "what's" of their organization. That's why management consultants typically organize a day when the CEO spends time in the field with customers. Just as peers need to stay connected to each other, leaders need to stay connected to each other and their larger community.

THE FOUR TYPES OF RITUALS

There are many types of rituals; some are led from the top, some are employee-driven. They can be company-wide, or a get-together for two. The only requirement is that they provide an opportunity to create or strengthen relationships. Each has its strengths and challenges.

1. EXPLICIT LARGE GROUP RITUALS

When I say large company get together I bet you thought holiday party. Those are great, but there are many ways to strengthen relationships company-wide. Let's think outside the punchbowl. Early in my career, I worked for a global design agency that always threw an amazing summer picnic. This all-fun no-work offsite went a long way toward breaking down barriers between departments and creating new relationships that transcend tenure, but infrequent budget-busters aren't the only option. Capital One's San Francisco-based design team hosts Tea Time every Friday afternoon at 3:30. (Don't be fooled; the tea cart is filled with beer and gin.) I happened to be there for one of these low-key end-of-the-week celebrations. This particular Friday, the conference room was the scene of a fierce Rock Band tournament on the company's PlayStation. With all the peripheral instruments available for anyone to try, I still think about the power this ridiculously fun and simple ritual had. Explicit large group rituals can even be asynchronous if you get creative. At Zappos, they set up a stage in the cafeteria with a bar stool and speakers for impromptu open mic lunches. If it is company-sponsored and reaches a lot of folks, the ritual falls into this quadrant.

WHAT YOU NEED

- A great idea that provides lots of opportunities for mingling

- A dedicated, possibly significant, budget

- The commitment to do it regularly

2. EXPLICIT SMALL GROUP RITUALS

Relationships can be built on a smaller scale, of course. A company-sponsored sports team is a classic ritual in this category. New hire coffee with the CEO or manager is also a terrific way to connect those of different departments and rank. I consulted with one financial technology startup in San Francisco that hosts regular lunch-and-learns. Employees are encouraged to sign up to share any skill or interest, but for their culture cooking is most popular. These have proven to be a great way for folks to connect around topics that interest them. Look for opportunities to attract smallish groups of people who want to be there, so they are open to new ideas and new people. Caution: requiring everyone to get together to learn the new time tracking system doesn't count.

WHAT YOU NEED

- Commitment to the ritual, so the day-to-day doesn't knock it off the list

- A dedicated, modest budget

- A way to communicate why and how this is happening

3. IMPLICIT SMALL GROUP RITUALS

Implicit rituals are those that happen without management instigation, and these are the small group behaviors that bloom organically. The regular lunch. The afternoon coffee. Groups of twos and threes are common to start, but it doesn't mean they can't grow. I know of one startup that supports a small group that likes to play music by setting aside a small office in which they can rehearse. The challenge with implicit small group rituals is that they can become insular—folks usually associate with those they know. Management should encourage teams to expand their circle and invite others to join them for coffee, a grilled cheese, or to rock out. If leadership can identify these naturally occurring rituals, they should do everything they can to support them.

WHAT YOU NEED

- An ear to help find these otherwise invisible rituals

- A willingness to support, and the restraint to not interrupt
- A way to encourage others to participate

4. IMPLICIT LARGE GROUP RITUALS

These are rituals that naturally spring from the culture and reach many people. I love the story of a massive engineering firm back East that, with instigation of one charismatic employee, started a daily jeopardy challenge that has brought together everyone within earshot for an opportunity to engage in a quick, playful morning ritual. It began with just two cube mates but has grown to a once-a-week trivia tournament held in the common space to accommodate everyone interested. It's regular, light-hearted, and fosters the kind of banter that naturally strengthens relationships. Implicit Large Group events are the queen of rituals: they are powerful because the creators feel ownership and enable the greatest cross-sampling of people. Bonus! These tend to be less expensive than the explicit large group, but just as effective.

WHAT YOU NEED

- Charismatic peer leader to initiate
- An eye to see the opportunity
- A willingness to support, and the restraint to not interrupt

WHAT EVERY GROWTH ORGANIZATION NEEDS

Relationship decay has been around since our primate ancestors began hunting in tribes; the blistering growth startups experience intensifies its symptoms and reveals its importance today. Growth organizations have to navigate too many challenges, of which culture is just one. But just like data analytics in the 2000s, managers, leaders, and executives need to turn serious attention toward rituals and invest in strengthening the connective tissue of their organization as it grows. What in the past may have been seen simply as perks and frivolous banter may in fact be the secret to success.

CREATING A CULTURE OF TRUST IN THE WORKPLACE

by Sue Bingham, HPWP Group

At a half-day seminar on trust by Franklin Covey, several hundred participants were asked to write down how their companies demonstrated trust with employees. Jack, the human resources director of a company that focused on creating a culture of high-performance, started writing right away and continued for the next three or four minutes. When he'd run out of steam, he looked around the room, only to see that others were having trouble writing much of anything. The Covey facilitator noticed him and asked him to share. Jack stood up.

"We are all salaried, including our production employees," he said. "The company trusts us to fulfill our responsibilities and pays accordingly. There are no time clocks. Our non-exempt team members who work overtime enter that time themselves in a system that goes directly to payroll. We have no set number of sick days for anyone; we never ask for doctor's notes or proof for bereavement. We expect and trust that people will come to work every day unless there is some necessary reason for them to be absent—in which case it's almost always paid.

"There are no locked supply cabinets or tool cribs. Everyone has a key that opens every door, even the front door." Jack smiled as he held up a small brass key. "We use key cards, of course, but we still give a regular key to every new employee as a symbol of our trust.

"The guys in our lab leave their wallets on the table, so whoever picks up for lunch for everyone can help themselves to the amount the coworker owes for their share. And when it comes to our work, we are trusted to solve problems and make decisions at all levels. Any line operator can shut down the line if he or she finds a problem."

He went on. "We have no guard gate and would never think of checking people's bags or car trunks as they leave the property. And as for security, our management realized some time ago that having 230 employees committed to protecting the company and its property was a lot better than a guard at a gate."

The facilitator started, "That's a good list…" Then Jack interrupted. "I'm not quite done." He continued to share the hard work his company invested in creating a culture of trust.

TRUST & REPORTING RELATIONSHIPS

Business trends—more people working remotely, baby boomers leaving the workforce—are raising the bar on the need for trust. Many traditional management and leadership practices, such as autocratic leadership styles and 9-to-5 work environments, are becoming obsolete.

However, many company cultures share an *unstated* belief that direct supervision of employees is the key to productivity. And there are a lot of misconceptions about a remote workforce, the biggest being that work won't get done at home. Managers fear that letting one person work from home will make others want to do the same. There's also the assumption that managing remote workers is too different from managing employees in person. The job is the same: All you need to do is use technology more creatively, be sensitive to people feeling isolated, and schedule regular communication.

These misconceptions center on a lack of trust, which leads to a desire for control. This can make leaders unreasonable. For example, one of our team members had a terrible commute at a former job. When she asked to come in earlier and leave earlier to reduce the hours of unproductive time that she spent in gridlock, she was told "no." They weren't willing to let her work from home, either, and they soon lost her as a result.

Because people know when they're most productive during the day, flexible work situations attract and retain talent, especially Millennials. In fact, 75 percent of Millennials[52] feel more productive working outside the office, but only about 43 percent get their wish. Remote working also greatly reduces turnover.[53]

When leaders trust employees to work from home, they feel empowered and trusted. They have the opportunity to be their own managers, which drives personal accountability. Fifty-nine percent[54] of Millennials say they are more productive when they have a flexible schedule, and 49 percent say they are happier this way. With high levels of trust, both flexible hours and remote working will lead to more productivity, not less.

---

[52] https://www2.deloitte.com/global/en/pages/about-deloitte/articles/millennialsurvey.html

[53] https://remote.co/10-stats-about-remote-work

[54] https://www.apqc.org/blog/four-myths-about-millennials-workplace-debunked

Of course, "remote" and "flexible" are two different issues. People might have a set schedule and work remotely, or they might report to the office but have a flexible schedule.

Flexibility is, inherently, an issue of fairness. Organizations regularly ask employees to remain "connected" while off work (evenings, weekends, and vacations), which most employees actually want to do. However, it's not fair to expect this of employees and not reciprocate in terms of flexibility of schedule when they're working in the office. Such expectations are too one-sided. While people will support and even own the need to be constantly connected, resentment will erode their motivation if the company doesn't provide flexibility in return.

Managing remotely is all about building mutual trust. Yet, decisions made in an attempt to mitigate a lack of trust don't always serve the organization regarding results.

Managers frequently require "activity" reporting. While some organizations use activities as lead measures for predicting results, other organizations use them to try to monitor performance. Sometimes companies rely on online or internet activity to monitor what's going on. Forty-three percent of U.S. employers[55] monitor their employees' emails, 45 percent focus on key logging, and 66 percent track the internet activity of their employees.

However, activity alone often doesn't reflect results. Most employees find activity reporting non-productive and a waste of time. Activity reporting communicates the not-so-subtle message that employees are not fully trusted to perform without needing to account for how they spend their time. Measure results instead. Leaders need to

---

[55] http://www.recruitingblogs.com/profiles/blogs/
how-do-big-companies-monitor-their-employees

remember that they hired a trusted adult, and they should continuously communicate with them about their progress.

Not trusting employees to perform out of sight makes hiring and retaining high-performance people a challenge in a rapidly declining labor pool.

CREATING A CULTURE OF TRUST

Establishing a trusting culture that will lead to high-performance must start with leadership. For leaders to feel comfortable in demonstrating trust, three things need to happen first.

Hire for trust as an attribute

Many companies say that hiring and promoting the best people is "job one," but often there are flaws in this system, such as overrating technical knowledge and emphasizing experience over character. These flaws are perpetuated with interviews that frequently don't include behaviorally based interview questions that can help define unknown personal attributes; a lack of in-depth reference checking; and failure to seriously consider feedback from one person on the interview team who has real reservations about a candidate.

Communicate trust as a value

Some companies place such a high value on trust that they have the same kind of *zero tolerance policy* for betraying trust as most companies have for working under the influence of drugs or alcohol. It starts with communicating the clear expectation that any violation of trust, no matter how small or large, is unacceptable. Once this expectation is very clear, anyone who violates trust loses their job.

In one incident, a long-term employee named Jimmy had worked at a highly respected company in Georgia for fifteen years. He was well known and liked by the management and owners. One day a team member, Scott, saw Jimmy take two reams of paper from the company supply room to his car. When Scott asked him what he was doing, Jimmy responded, "Let's just say you didn't see this." Scott had a dilemma. If he looked the other way, he was minimizing Jimmy's action.

For team members in a high-trust culture, reporting this kind of incident is expected. Management was visibly upset the day Jimmy was terminated, but there was no outcry from fellow team members, as might be expected. Some had their suspicions, but this was the first time a violation of this sort had come to light. After he left, Jimmy asked the company to post a letter he wrote to everyone apologizing for his betrayal. He urged fellow team members to value the freedom and security they had in working for this kind of company, and cautioned them never to do anything as stupid as what he had done.

As soon as people start to muddy the water, saying, "but it was just a little white lie," or "it wasn't that big of a deal," there is no longer zero tolerance. A zero-tolerance policy creates a workplace where everyone can leave personal property unlocked and company tools and equipment openly accessible. It also expands the responsibility for safety and security to every person who works there, and people take it seriously. There is an extremely high level of pride in being part of this type of organization.

Address the 5 percent, not the 95 percent

In my experience, only 5 percent of employees put in minimal effort and take unethical shortcuts. The other 95 percent are responsible adults who take pride in their work.

Even in the most trusting of environments, there may still be instances of theft or deceit. It is important not to let the bad apple that has slipped by your selection process dictate how you treat the majority of your trustworthy adults. Avoid the following:

- Requiring all employees to carry transparent purses/bags or do trunk checks. If the company believes it must have a guard gate, expect the guard to act as an ambassador for the company and be welcoming as people come and go—visitors and employees alike.
- Installing internal cameras or trying to trap people. If there is a problem of theft, publicly acknowledge the occurrence, asking for everyone's help in solving the issue while simultaneously reinforcing the company's belief in the integrity of the workforce. When trust is a clearly established value, team members will hold each other accountable.
- Overreacting to an instance of theft. Acknowledge it happened, but reinforce that it is not going to keep the company from maintaining faith in the integrity of its workforce.
- Letting an act of mistrust change company behavior or policies. Use it to reinforce trusting behaviors.

HOW LEADERS TAKE THE RISK

It's a leadership responsibility to take risks, use judgment, and operate from positive motives. No one wants to be fooled or viewed as naïve, but if leaders want to create a trusting workplace, it must start with them.

- Look at how locked doors, tool cribs, and supply cabinets communicate a lack of trust in everyone—not just a few.

- Evaluate company policies. Do they require an employee's signature on documents (even employee handbooks) so that the company feels more legally protected if a policy is violated and the employee claims not to know the policies? Does the company require documentation to prove that an illness was valid or the funeral attendance real?
- Engage and empower people to solve problems and make decisions. They're adults. They solve problems outside the workplace all the time.

When companies show trust and respect by eliminating the actions intended to protect them, they will see loyalty, dedication, and higher performance from those most critical to the company's success.

ASSESSING YOUR OWN TRUST ORIENTATION

To know your orientation to trust others, ask yourself:

Do people need to earn my trust?

Or,

Do I generally trust people until they demonstrate they can't be trusted?

Whichever question you answered "yes" or "no" to is simply a reflection of your life experiences. If you grew up in an overpopulated city where crime was more common, you learned to lock your doors and be wary of strangers. If you grew up in the countryside where everyone knew one another, you probably left your keys in the car without a thought.

So why does your personal orientation to trust matter? It matters because it may drive your assumptions about people, or certain groups of people. And your assumptions drive your behavior.

Also, in your personal life and your work life, you may have encountered people who have taken advantage of you, and these painful experiences can make you cynical. For managers, that cynicism can manifest as negative assumptions: employees are lazy, they are incapable of directing their own behavior, or they lack integrity. Managers who hold negative assumptions tend toward micromanaging, locking up needed supplies, withholding important information, and creating senseless rules and policies, causing even the best people to lose passion for what they do.

Years ago I worked with an executive who told me he wanted his employees to act like owners—but he refused to give keys to plant workers who arrived before the office staff. He wasn't making a positive assumption that employees could be trusted to enter and exit the building as they pleased. How were they supposed to feel ownership if they weren't even allowed a key to the building?

To demonstrate positive assumptions, show that you reject micromanaging. Give challenging assignments with the clear and confident belief that your expectations will be met. And promote transparency. Don't hide information based on the assumption that people will mishandle it. (Try adding a "through the grapevine" agenda item to meetings as a fun, informal way for people to share company information they've heard so you can either confirm it or debunk the rumor.)

When managers demonstrate positive assumptions, employees respond in kind. A management action or decision that might normally be questioned or unpopular is accepted because employees trust that there is more to the story. This will provide everyone with a level of comfort during times of rapid change and growth.

THE BOTTOM LINE

Creating trusting relationships, developing a workplace where trust is a basic expectation, and being aware of how your own trust orientation drives your behaviors are requirements for the changes happening now and the dramatic changes that are forecast for the future. Be an exemplary leader by creating trust through your thoughts, words, and actions. High trust adds exponentially to positive business results—the lack of it only adds to costs.

THE AGE OF THE SELF-MANAGED ORGANIZATION

by Doug Kirkpatrick, Nufocus Strategic Group

I s it possible for talented employees to manage themselves— without bosses, titles, or command authority—and experience high-performance combined with happiness? Apparently, the answer is yes. There are serious and successful vanguard organizations now blazing self-management trails of full engagement, lean bureaucracy and lofty business performance.

Self-management is the absence (or sharp limitation) of formal hierarchy. Each member of the organization assumes the traditional functions of a manager (planning, coordinating, controlling, staffing, and directing). They are personally responsible for forging their relationships, planning their work, coordinating their actions with others, acquiring the resources they need to accomplish their mission, and for taking corrective action with other members when needed. Self-management is a formula for engagement. It's also a formula for accountability: in a truly transparent self-managed enterprise, there is no place to hide.

Traditional management relies significantly on command authority. Rightly or wrongly, that's the fastest way to get things done through other people. Command authority, defined as the authority to direct the activities of others with the expectation that one's direction will be obeyed, is binary. You either possess command authority or you don't. The question then becomes: in what circumstances should command authority even exist? It's possible for an organization to be relatively self-managed overall while preserving limited command authority for predetermined situations. Organizational leaders should be thoughtful about the existence and scope of command authority. Imagine a spectrum of possibilities ranging from extreme command authority (once represented by institutional slavery) to total self-management (zero command authority). Given the accelerating pace of disorienting technological change, where should twenty-first century organizations wish to locate on the spectrum?

Making the leap from traditional management to principle-centered organizational self-management positively impacts people engagement, collective intelligence, business performance, the management tax (direct and indirect costs of bureaucracy), and altruism (meaning, it's the right thing to do).

Tomato giant Morning Star created a unique organizational system based on core principles of human interaction. Position power and titles don't exist at Morning Star. Everyone has an equal voice in matters that affect them. There is no unilateral authority to promote, discipline, or fire. Acquiring or concluding the services of other colleagues must be accomplished according to a clear set of established principles incorporating due process. There is as much need for leadership in a self-managed organization as in a hierarchical one; it's just that self-managed leadership is dynamic rather than static—it depends on the issue and the individuals. It is earned. Leadership can rotate and evolve naturally, depending on the circumstances. No particular leadership style is required, and many leadership styles can work well.

A principle is a fundamental truth from which others are derived. Human principles are not unlike physical principles (for example, gravity). Principles exist, and they're always working. People can choose to align their behavior with fundamental principles or not, but choosing to ignore principles (like gravity) can have serious consequences. Similarly, choosing to ignore human principles (like respect for the voluntary nature of human interaction and keeping commitments) can cause enormous damage. Notorious examples abound: consider Charles Ponzi fraudulently promising investors unrealistic arbitrage returns.

While ignoring basic human principles carries serious costs, aligning actions with principles conveys significant benefits.

Organizational self-management isn't a fad. In addition to Morning Star, pioneers and innovators like Semco, Valve, Vagas, Menlo Innovations, Meetup, Gore, Buurtzorg, Haier, and others have paved the way—each with its own unique approach.

SELF-MANAGEMENT IS FRACTAL MANAGEMENT

The world is becoming more complex. Some reports indicate that human knowledge is doubling every thirteen months. Atul Gawande, author of *The Checklist Manifesto*, writes that with over thirteen thousand ways for the human body to fail, medicine today is the art of mastering complexity, if it can be mastered at all. Complexity is a constant of modern organizational life.

The path to managing complexity is, paradoxically, through simplicity. Simple principles act as an enterprise constitution, allowing for concentrated human effort. The fixed nature of the principles will enable people to exercise effective autonomy in a fluid environment. This foundation allows people to freely act with agility and speed in response to dynamic change. It's easier to hit a target with arrows fired from the bedrock of principle than from the quivering quicksand of a corporate makeover or C-suite politics. The chain of command theory made sense when information moved at the speed of Morse code. Today, chains of command forged in pursuit of the mirage of control are shackling business performance everywhere.

A networked organization is highly adaptable. Self-managed peers connect with each other by voluntary agreement, not by occupying a box on an organization chart. When these individual agreements are digitally rendered and relationally plotted, they might resemble a vast spider web, with random connections running everywhere. If one were to make a time-lapse movie of such a diagram, it would change shape and size as individuals enter and exit the ecosystem or dynamically reconfigure their relationships and commitments.

Spider silk, by weight, is five times stronger than steel. Human networks, like spider webs, are tough and resilient. When someone leaves a network of self-managers, the remaining members quickly organize to reallocate roles and responsibilities. A self-managing human network is like a self-healing organism. It may bend but rarely breaks.

A fractal is a complex geometric pattern exhibiting self-similarity in that small details of structure viewed at any scale repeat elements of the overall pattern. Regardless of the degree of magnification used to view a network diagram of a self-managed enterprise, whether at the level of the individual (a single node), the factory or business unit (a sub-group of nodes), or the entire enterprise (all nodes), core principles are present and operating. One also finds the functions of management (planning, organizing, staffing, coordinating, controlling) at every degree of magnification, because in self-management, everyone is a manager. There are no titles, bosses, VPs, supervisors, or hierarchy of any kind. There is only work and people who engage in work. The fluidity of this arrangement enables individual and enterprise agility—a critical success factor in a complex world where information moves at the speed of light.

In a self-managed ecosystem, every peer voluntarily engages with the mission and principles of the enterprise. The cultural DNA of respect for principle is deeply embedded in the organization through language, education, modeling, and practice. This cultural reinforcement reduces the risk of individuals or groups acting in ways incongruent with the mission, vision, values, or principles.

Since there are no inherent barriers to communication anywhere in a network, free-flowing information catalyzes operational decision-making everywhere. A further powerful benefit of self-management is that innovation can and does arise from any point in the network. Individual self-managers freely propose process improvements and innovations to their peers. Good ideas always have a fighting chance for implementation.

Similarly, each peer in a self-managed organization has an equal voice concerning decisions that affect them. Self-management is not about voting or majority rule. It's about comprehensive due process and protecting the voice of every member of the enterprise. Every peer is a stakeholder in decisions that impact their work and is free to engage in the decision-making process. Do peer-reviewed decisions often take longer to make than those in a traditional management structure? Absolutely. Is decision quality better with relatively greater input? Definitely.

Will organizational self-management lead to a loss of control, or even chaos? One possible answer may be found in another question: who is more likely to spot a threat or an opportunity in the work environment—a manager who inspects the workplace a few times a day, or colleagues who are working side by side with each other all day long, and have the freedom and responsibility to speak up and be heard? There is an opportunity for much greater organizational control, not less, when everyone is a manager.

SELF-MANAGEMENT IS SCALABLE

According to a recent article in *BBC Earth News*, scientists recently discovered an ant mega-colony that apparently has colonized much of the world, rivaling humans in the sheer scale of its global domination. The Argentine ant (*Linepithema humile*) mega-colony originated in South America but now spans much of the Mediterranean region, California, and western Japan—one super-colony apparently covers six thousand kilometers of Mediterranean coastline. The ants' chemical hydrocarbon signatures provided proof of the common identity of separate colonies existing on multiple continents.

These Argentine world travelers have a simple, two-pronged mission. First, they seek to survive; and second, to reproduce. Their mission, which they execute to perfection, is the essence of simplicity. As long as they focus on the mission, there are no apparent barriers to scale.

Ants use chemical signals to provide actionable feedback and facilitate coordination. Self-managed professionals use information systems to provide feedback and coordinate activities and adjust their "paths" accordingly. Ant colonies use division of labor to feed themselves and modify their environments. Self-managed colleagues freely agree to act in concert with others or work individually. Individual

ants take the initiative in seeking food and shelter, chemi-
cally communicating promising trails to their fellow ants.
Self-managed colleagues take the initiative and create buy-in
for their ideas and innovations. It's challenging to identify
the leaders of an ant mega-colony—or of a self-managed
organization.

Leadership is fluid—and depends on the flow of commitments back and forth between the organization's members.
If it's possible to grow without human bosses from zero to
become the world's largest player in a global industry, as
Morning Star did, then there are no *inherent* barriers to
scale for a self-managed human enterprise.

Identifying sources of strategic competitive advantage
is an existential challenge for any organization. Simple yet
powerful organizational designs informed by the natural
world provide tantalizing models of sustainable strategic
advantage.

OTHER PRACTICES FROM THE NATURAL WORLD

Ken Thompson's book *Bioteams: High-performance Teams
Based on Nature's Most Successful Designs* describes how to
create high-performance teams based on examples found
in the natural world. As he notes in the first chapter, "after
[nature's] 3.8 billion years of research and development,
failures are fossils, and what surrounds us is the secret to
survival. Like the viceroy butterfly imitating the monarch,
we humans are imitating the best and brightest organisms
in our habitat."

The idea of biomimetics began, Thompson observes,
in the 1940s when a Swiss inventor noticed how certain
plant seeds clung to his clothing. Closer examination led
to the discovery of a unique hook-and-loop mechanism,
which led to the invention of Velcro. From that point, it

was only a matter of time before theorists began to think more deeply about how to adapt nature's designs for human use. Thompson observes that bioteaming is simply the application of biomimetics to group effectiveness in human organizations.

What better opportunity to apply the lessons of bioteaming than to a self-managed organization, where individual members enjoy a large quantum of autonomy in pursuit of their respective missions? Absent the friction of bureaucracy and hierarchy, these organizations should be uniquely equipped to avail themselves of the best analogies that nature has to offer. There are plenty to choose from.

From the ant world, we learn about the power of instant short-burst, whole-group broadcast communication. Ants communicate both opportunity (food) and threat (predator) messages through whole-group chemical broadcasts. These short messages require no response (eliminating the need for two-stage communication), and trigger message receivers to act instantly. Efficient and effective.

Short-burst communication is not only efficient and effective, it's also lucrative. In a round of funding announced on April 1, 2016, fast-growing workplace collaboration startup Slack (so named because it helped founder Stewart Butterfield and his employees communicate with less tension) was valued at $3.8 billion. Butterfield says his goal is to end "interoffice email" because it's a less efficient system than messaging. Competitors have taken notice. Companies like Chatwork, Ryver, HipChat, Lua, and Switch are all vying for a piece of the growing collaborative workspace pie—and changing the nature of work.

Thompson notes that traditional organizations rely heavily on permission structures to protect against mistakes by individual members. Bioteams, on the other hand, obliterate those structures and drive accountability through transparency and reliance on reputation. Accountability then becomes the natural consequence of bioteaming, not an artifact of hierarchical authority structures.

Bioteaming principles, according to Thompson, include the following:

- Self-Management. Individuals react and collaborate in response to information, not command-and-control orders.

- Non-Verbal Communication. Team members do not rely on face-to-face communication but work asynchronously across geographic locations and time zones. Verbal communication is fine, when possible, but not necessary to achieve goals.

- Bias for Action. Team members problem-solve and learn through rapid, evolutionary experimentation and feedback. As individuals, they have concrete goals but no fixed strategies for achieving them. When something works, it's communicated, reinforced, and embedded in the collective set of responses to the next challenge. When something doesn't work, it simply dies. The key to success is being experimental, not prescriptive.

- Three Dimensions. Team members thrive best when they relate to their fellow team members, their organization as a whole, and the external environment. Web-based collaboration technologies (like Slack and its competitors) can support connectivity with all three dimensions—creating more effective team members.

- Motivation and Conflict. Bees, ants, birds, and microbes simply react and respond to stimuli—they have no choice in the matter. Human beings are different—they have the power to choose their response in any given situation. There are lots of ways to support individual effectiveness in the workplace of the future: coaching, mentoring, facilitation, mediation, skill building, and more. Myriad books, programs, methodologies, and consultancies are dedicated to these disciplines—all focused on helping team members make the most effective choices about time, talent, resources, and relationships.

- Individuality. One member's mistake in a beehive or an ant colony doesn't really matter—there are thousands of peers doing the same thing. On a human team, aberrant behavior or gross incompetence is a huge and potentially destructive deal. (Imagine boarding a commercial airline flight with "pilot" Frank Abegnale, Jr., the notorious con man featured in the movie *Catch Me if You Can*!) Peer accountability and transparency are crucial to mitigating the risk of individual failure.

- Human Intelligence. As Thompson notes, a principle of biological teams is that complex group behavior can arise from simple individual behavior given sufficient time, scale, and feedback loops. Well-coordinated human teams can produce dazzling results even if the individuals aren't dazzling by themselves. That's the power of bioteaming.

The founder of the 5,900-member Employee Engagement Network, David Zinger, launched a three-year study of honeybees to distill powerful lessons for human organizations. In his e-book *Waggle: 39 Ways to Improve Human Organizations, Work, and Engagement*, he notes the need for incessant collaboration and the need to stay connected with one's organization.

Zinger also shares a link to a YouTube video called the "The Waggle Dance of the Honeybee" from the Georgia Tech College of Computing. Research demonstrates that bee collaboration is incredibly sophisticated and mathematically precise, enabling individual bees to independently fly to food sources at great distances with astonishing efficiency. With tools like Slack and over one million words available in the English language, one would think that humans should be able to collaborate effectively even without waggle dancing.

The power and elegance of bioteaming is indisputable. Whether organizational leaders will detach themselves from the perceived security blanket of traditional, artificial hierarchy to fully experience that power is another question.

COLLECTIVE INTELLIGENCE, SOCIAL TECHNOLOGIES, AND ORGANIZING FOR SUCCESS

Natural systems harvest, rebroadcast, and amplify individual member messages and format those messages for collective action. The intelligence of the group is far more powerful than the intelligence of any given member. Social technologies that unlock group intelligence for effective response are important tools of the self-managed organizations of the future.

James Surowiecki, author of *The Wisdom of Crowds*, shares the tale of the hunt for USS Scorpion, a nuclear submarine that disappeared in May 1968 somewhere in the North Atlantic. Based on the last radio contact, the Navy began searching a radius twenty miles wide, a nearly hopeless task. Fortunately, naval officer John Craven had a better idea. He concocted a multitude of potential scenarios and then compiled a team with a diverse range of skills and backgrounds. He asked the team members to give their best individual guesses regarding Scorpion's fate and place bets on the likelihood of each scenario with bottles of Chivas Regal as prizes. Craven built a composite scenario built on all the guesses. Five months after Scorpion's disappearance, this intelligence, built on the collective wisdom of Craven's team, enabled a navy ship to find Scorpion 220 yards from where the group (but no individual group member) predicted it would be.

Like the quantum computers of the future, where one relatively small quantum machine could have more computing power than all conventional computers combined, quantum organizations will creatively and effectively deploy crowdsourcing, gamification, voice activation, collective intelligence, and myriad other social technologies to let people bring their entire brains to work. As Chuck Blakeman wrote in *Inc.* magazine: "In the Participation Age, which is already upon us, everybody is getting their brain back, and work once again is becoming a meaningful, integrated part of our lives, not something we put up with to make money."

The benefits of participation are real: in the book *Firms of Endearment: How World-Class Companies Profit From Passion and Purpose*, the authors examine how to build high-performance companies on love, involving all stakeholders (all of whom, coincidentally, happen to be human beings). They found that humanistic firms of endearment (FoEs) maximize value to society as a whole, not just to shareholders, by creating emotional, experiential, social, and financial value. Publicly held FoEs returned 1,026 percent for investors over the ten years ending June 30, 2006, compared with 122 percent for the S&P 500. FoE Costco, for example, pays people 40 percent more than Sam's Club, yet generates significantly more profit per employee.

Powerful social technologies are finding their way into companies and organizations around the world. Open Space, detailed by discoverer Harrison Owen in his book *Open Space Technology: A User's Guide*, has been practiced in over 100,000 different meetings in 160 countries, involving self-organizing groups of between five and 2,100 participants. In a safe, diverse Open Space environment, participants self-organize and grapple with the burning issues most important to them, where collective wisdom can emerge. Owen once facilitated a powerful Open Space in Rome in 2002 with fifty Israelis and Palestinians.

The World Café, a process to facilitate large-group dialogue discovered by Juanita Brown and David Isaacs in 1995, has also found resonance around the world as a social technology to drive multi-stakeholder engagement. The World Café publishes an Impact Map that displays its influence in communities, corporations, government and public institutions around the world.

Rod Collins, former chief operating executive of the Blue Cross Blue Shield Federal Employee Program and author of *Wiki Management: A Revolutionary New Model for a Rapidly Changing and Collaborative World*, shares an exercise he calls the Elegant Set, a method of quickly aggregating the collective intelligence in a room of diverse stakeholders. Keith McCandless and Henri Lipmanowicz, co-authors of *The Surprising Power of Liberating Structures: Simple Rules to Unleash A Culture of Innovation*, describe several simple, yet powerful, exercises designed to unleash innovation and performance through engagement.

To the degree they are deployed, liberating social technologies will exert tectonic pressure on traditional organizations to, well, liberate people. Once exposed to these technologies, people will expect to have a voice and will expect their voices to be heard. Given the typically low employee engagement levels measured by numerous researchers, it would appear that organizations have little to lose—and much to gain—by listening. Organizations, like honeybees, must learn to pay attention to the "waggle dances" of individual members or risk missing out on serendipitous opportunities—or avoiding unanticipated risks.

Patents expire, trade secrets leak, talent walks, and technology is largely fungible. Superior methods of organizing and managing, however, represent an astronomical and generally untapped source of sustainable business advantage. In an age when information freely gushes everywhere on luminous rivers of light, the future belongs to organizations that can engage every member with freedom, principle, and purpose.

BEYOND EMOTIONAL INTELLIGENCE TO WHOLE-BODY WISDOM

by Anna McGrath, Godfrey Dadich Partners

I woke up at 1:14 a.m. the morning this chapter was to go to the editor. I had completed the original version of the chapter a few weeks earlier. My mind was fine with that—but my body was in revolt.

And even though my mind does the writing, my body was telling me I had something more important to convey. It was communicating to me through what I call whole-body wisdom, or WBW. The wisdom of my body woke me up in the middle of the night to something I had been ignoring.

It is well established that our bodies and our minds are connected and in constant communication with one another. What we refer to as "gut instinct" is based on an emotional response that manifests as physical sensations in our stomachs. It is not a weird phrase—it is a legitimate phenomenon that reflects how we experience emotion, process those experiences and signals, and translate them into emotional intelligence. And my body was telling me: *It's time to re-negotiate every agreement on the table and what everyone expects from you and start over*. That sounds crazy, right?

83

SLAM ON THE BRAKES

That early morning, my whole-body wisdom shouted at me, "No!" My mind was pleading: "Just let it go as is, the deadline is here, the editor needs to do their thing. Don't mess with your fellow collaborators' and buddies' timelines; this is selfish." But every other part of my body— through my WBW—was ordering me to slam on the brakes!

Whole-body wisdom isn't for sissies. It demands you be brave enough to face what you are thinking, feeling, and intuiting in an integrated way. It asks you to overcome all the external messages that say to ignore your body's pointed messages to you.

Society appears to reward us for following the pack, compromising, and casting aside whatever is too "different." But if we override the messages our body is sending, we create a jangle inside ourselves, and that can lead to disaster. Reflect on all the stories of public humiliation you read in the media, the nightmare cultures that some leaders create, and even some aspects of your life you would not like others to write about.

These crises often have roots in a bodily experience that the person ignores, likely interpreting that sensation as messy or irrelevant. Others, instead of ignoring a WBW communication, overreact. They lash out passive aggressively instead of acknowledging that they feel wounded by a careless remark and are unable to deal with the emotions surging through them.

The fastest route to misery is overriding, ignoring, or misinterpreting your precious whole-body wisdom. It requires practice to learn what your body is telling you. Our bodies send us messages, or what I like to call "data packets." The data emerges in our heads, hearts, guts, and whole-body experiences. Whole-body wisdom comes from noticing the data, gaining insight from it, taking action in alignment with it, and then integrating that experience into your decision-making matrix.

This chapter is designed to cover the importance of creating healthy lives, cultures, and organizations which apply to an individual, team, and organization-wide level. The areas we will explore together are WBW practices, response-agility, and conscious commitments. Based on the transformation work of Kathlyn and Gay Hendricks of the Hendricks Institute[56], I have developed many practices, workshops, and materials in collaboration with them. I am forever grateful for the impact they have had on me and the lives of my friends and clients.

WHOLE-BODY WISDOM: PRACTICE MAKES HEALTHY

Rewrite the chapter. Don't rewrite the chapter. It's good enough… NO, IT IS NOT!

My mind and my body relayed contradictory messages to me. I listened to my heart, gut, and whole integrated body. I could feel the churning in my belly. My heart raced, and I felt a tightness in my chest.

Yes, Anna, you feel scared and sad.

What was I afraid of? Immediately, I had the thought that I was scared of making extra work for the editors by turning in a rushed, unpolished product. The delay might negatively impact my fellow collaborators the longer it took for me to turn it in. These thoughts and sensations were

---

[56]   Kathlyn Hendricks is a brilliant Body Intelligence teacher, friend, and a one-of-a-kind master facilitator who wrote a number of books including *Conscious Loving Ever After* along with her husband, Gay Hendricks. He is also a prolific writer (including *Big Leap*) and a fellow genius "cut through to the root cause of the issue" magician. https://www.hendricks.com/about

stirring a pot of emotion inside me. Turning in the chapter as-is was the easy route; however, I wanted to submit my best work. I would never be able to look at the book without knowing I had copped out.

Each of these experiences—whether thoughts, sensations, or feelings—were "data packets" guiding me toward the ideal outcome. If I accept they are messages sent to guide me, how am I supposed to interpret them? Well, I've spent over fifteen years practicing my noticing skills and creating a body map of *yes* and *no*. I have in the past ignored the *no* messages I was receiving. I eventually learned that every time I do, the messages become louder until there is only one logical course of action. Even worse, the longer I leave the issue, the greater the pain and negative outcome.

When my body sent me an urgent message at 1:14 am, I knew everything about this chapter needed to change, and it was time to get writing. I needed to renegotiate my agreements with my fellow collaborators, and I felt scared. But I was committed to taking action. All of this became clear to me in the moment I began to pay attention to my body sensations.

THE WISDOM IN A "FULL-BODY YES"

How many times have you set a goal and worked toward that outcome, but along the way, new data emerges? The data is integrated into the work in iterative cycles, and *voilà*, you have a finished product. Or you ignore the data and you experience a minor glitch as a result—like a lack of resonance in our writing or a disagreement with a loved one.

However, sometimes ignoring data brings significant challenges—like in 2008, when homebuyers thought that housing prices would keep rising. Then the US housing bubble burst.

I remember my internal excitement when my loft increased in price in the early 2000s, the feeling of flow and upward rising energy. If something seems too good to be true, it more than likely is (unless it's whole-body wisdom). A few things happened toward the end of 2006, and my body started sending me louder and louder messages. I felt it when my fellow homeowner association members chose not to buy earthquake insurance on our building in the San Francisco South of Market liquefaction zone. It was enough to wipe out any breath I had in my body when someone casually said, "Don't worry; whoever is last to leave the building just needs to toss a match to set light to the building." (Then they could claim on homeowners insurance.) I felt it again when escalating housing prices seemed to be disconnecting from reality. My body sent even stronger signals of anxiety because I was just three years into owning a new business. These sensations combine into worrying thoughts—what I call "future fears"—and are a complete waste of time. When people would talk about the "big one," I experienced sensations in my body that I would label as sadness, anger, and fear. I knew an earthquake that impacted my uninsured loft could wipe out twenty years of work. Is it time to leave? My body responded with what I call a "full-body YES." So my wife and I sold up and became renters for a few years.

When your whole-body wisdom lines up, and there are no more jangles to explore and process, you experience a "full-body YES." I have asked thousands of clients and audiences at conferences to tune into their whole-body aliveness. Some have built this capacity, and others think I am speaking a foreign language. I am! It is the language of whole-body wisdom.

My "full-body YES" decision to sell the loft triggered a series of other decisions. We moved to the coast, where we have the privilege of seeing the Pacific Ocean every day and whales in June through September. Thanks, whole-body wisdom!

Did John Taylor, president of the nonprofit National Community Reinvestment Coalition, listen to his WBW? He warned Congress about the predatory and fraudulent lending that was fueling a housing bubble as early as 2000. "We brought it to the attention of both Democrats and Republicans," Taylor told CNN ten years after the crash. "In the end, it took the nation's economy having to collapse before they felt the need to do something… thinking about it now, I can feel myself being angry about it," Taylor said[57], reflecting on what I suggest was his whole-body wisdom.

Distractions can slow us down and prevent us from receiving those important WBW messages. And the costs can be significant. I was writing this chapter at the same time I was negotiating the acquisition of my company, WonderWorks Consulting, to a fabulous client, Godfrey Dadich Partners. I was swimming in complexities and a sea of distractions from my WBW and the pending deadline. And, while I make no excuses, I live by the wisdom of my body—and I still missed its signals.

In my experience, individuals who rush through life ignoring their bodies' needs and their WBW messages have a greater likelihood of creating poor outcomes, including greater stress from constant activity and lack of rest and relaxation. This leads to many health impacts, including heart disease, hypertension, and lack of cell repair through-out your body due to the impact of stress.[58] Without WBW

---

[57] https://lite.cnn.com/en/
article/h_ee387040a10aded30a68c5d7ad1f1edb
[58] *Behave: The Biology of Humans at Our Best and Worst* by Robert Sapolsky. This excellent book provides numerous research studies from a wide variety of disciplines that impact the way we behave including: psychology, sociology, neurobiology, and primatology.

and making decisions using full-body yeses, all that is left is compromise, disconnection, and dis-ease.

Living in alignment with WBW starts with being present and making similarly aligned decisions. To make effective decisions, it is essential to gather all the data—external reports, research, colleagues' or clients' feedback—and then process it with your WBW, not only your mind. Too often, people override what they want and go along with the group when it is not the best solution for the organization, instead of speaking up and sharing the insights derived from their WBW. Once you commit to connecting with that, the next step is to commit to being authentic with others.

The minute I became clear about this chapter and what I wanted to write about, I experienced my "full-body YES," and felt a big surge of energy, a renewed commitment to writing, and the flow of content to match. I could feel the difference between version one and two. As I started to write, I felt excited. I now had the energy and commitment to change my agreements, face the potential feelings of my collaborators, and write something that resonated with me and, therefore, would have the opportunity to resonate with others.

RESPONSE-AGILITY: HOW TO STAY NIMBLE

The pace of change is outstripping our ability to transform. To keep up, we need to increase our capacity to respond with agility. A "response-agility" framework is required—not just for the sake of our organizations, but for the sake of humanity, our ecosystem, our whole planet.

So, what is Response-Agility?[59]

---

[59] Response-Agility was coined in collaboration with Audrey Hazekamp, founder of Tall Poppy, Inc., as we were writing about this subject and deepening our whole-body wisdom practices.

Think of it as awareness in action. It is the ability to respond instead of reacting, and it requires being alert to your WBW. It is a way to learn and grow your capacity to respond with agility.

There are two ways to interact with the world: respond or react. Are you consciously responding or unconsciously reacting? We respond when we are present, awake, and integrating our whole-body wisdom. We react when we perceive an attack. We fall back on coping mechanisms like defensiveness, inauthentically accommodating others, or avoiding a situation altogether.

One indicator of a high level of response-agility is how quickly an individual can shift from a reactive state to a constructive, authentic response after being triggered. Let's explore this example:

You've received an email from a colleague repeating a conversation you just had with them about an issue you disagree on. They copied two colleagues in your organization and a client. As you read, your blood starts to boil. You feel judged and subtly accused of being the problem. Your immediate lizard-brain reaction is to fire off a scorching email and finish the war in one campaign. The adult who is skilled in whole-body wisdom practices would take a different approach. Maybe they first stand up and move some energy by going to get a glass of water. Or if they have a friend at work, they may choose to exaggerate their reactions in a mime of their experience. The point is to move your body to move your energy.

An indicator of your level of "response-agility" in that email moment would be how quickly you move through the experience and respond in a way that is aligned to your purpose, while taking healthy responsibility for the inter-action and offering a next action to create a clearing and/or completion for you and/or the other person. That could sound like: "I felt scared and angry after reading your email. I would appreciate speaking with you via video conference when you are available so I can own how I set this situation up. I'd also like to hear what you have discovered on your end. I predict we'll look back on this incident in years to come and laugh, and that's not my current experience. I intend to create a win for all as we resolve this situation and any unexpressed emotions."

When you respond in this way, taking healthy responsibility, it opens up a space to be present, connect with yourself, and then with the other person, while you share what you each experienced.

A great question in these situations is, "Is it funny yet?" If the answer is no, then it is time to own your reaction. You are unconsciously committed to being at the effect of others, of situations, of circumstances. You are saying, "I experience life as a victim."

The conscious commitment would be: "I commit to owning my experiences and outcomes." This is healthy responsibility. Once ownership and taking healthy responsibility are practiced reliably, people grow a response-agility capacity. Many organizations, including those that *overly* emphasize servant leadership and customer-centric practices, can sometimes neglect the value of self.

If we don't have a grounded, healthy "I" as we navigate the working world, it is possible to get lost in someone else's unhealthy "we." Whole-body wisdom and response-agility starts with the "I" and then moves to the "we."

The response-agility quotient of each stakeholder in an organization will eventually be the key metric and differentiator for organizations. This capability is essential to navigate the unknown future with a sense of ease instead of creating drama and low-level panic as the increasing pace of change turns everything we thought we knew upside down.

"Never again will the pace of change be as slow as it is today," said Stan Sthanunathan, Unilever's SVP of Consumer & Marketing Insights. People are expected to be increasingly nimble as they collaborate with teams of interdisciplinary geniuses that aim to find the magical answers to pressing and extremely complex issues. Working in our current reality without WBW and response-agility would be like Edison trying to invent electricity in a basement with no access to lightning.

When people are changing out their personal operating system, the immediate response is a combination of one or more of the following: excitement, fear, and resistance. Their response-agility quotient is tested, and again at a much deeper level soon after making any commitment to change—whether it is immediately or after a month.

If someone has been working toward being a manager for decades, say, and suddenly the organization no longer has managers, that will be a major upheaval for them.[60] Some will be excited on day one or even day ninety, as they have not yet absorbed the implications of how they will need to change the way they operate on a fundamental level. This type of inner transformation will not be solved by technical training or mind-centric solutions alone.

I suggest starting with response-agility practices. Let's take a look at the building blocks of this practice:

- Noticing, which builds your awareness capacity

- Awareness, which builds deeper understanding

---

[60] Self-organizing systems and structures. Anna McGrath is a licensed Holacracy provider and in 2012 was the first in the USA. Holacracy is a system and structure—a hierarchy of roles (not people) that is based on a constitution. *Holacracy: The New Management System for a Rapidly Changing World* by Brian J. Robertson

- Understanding, which builds knowledge
- Knowledge, which builds awareness of what you don't know
- Awareness of what you don't know, which builds curiosity and openness to discovery
- Openness to discovery, which opens up the world of possibility and magic

In the middle of that amazing list are feelings—data packets of body wisdom to guide us on our journeys—and so often they are ignored. This creates pain, unease, and distraction from fulfilling our potential. Ignored feelings can cause physical as well as mental distress.

If the list above is what helps build response-agility, what are the things that undermine it?

- Wanting to be the smartest person in the room
- Believing there is only one solution: my solution
- Becoming a villain, victim, or a self-appointed hero who tries to temporarily smooth over a tense situation in an attempt to avoid experiencing feelings
- Being unable to process fear, anger, and sadness
- Defending against feedback from colleagues, clients, and partners
- Failing to recognize that we are collaborating with the universe all the time and that we may even be choosing to create conflicts and negative outcomes
- Thinking that learning is for other people and that you've learned all you need

- Remaining silent about challenges and ideas in meetings or to those they perceive have "the power"

- Gossiping and complaining about others rather than speaking to the person directly

- Moving decision-making upward in the organization versus where the work is performed

CONSCIOUS COMMITMENTS: THE GUIDEPOSTS FOR YOUR JOURNEY

I believe in the power of both/and. Difference is the heart of diversity, and diametrically opposed perspectives are valuable and beneficial. Both/and means honoring these opposite positives. Diverse ideas and perspectives are a source of strength for an organization when we harness the energy and power embedded in positive opposites. Thinking and feeling, transformation and continuity, structure and behaviors; these are inverse positives. So is technology and whole-body wisdom.[61]

It would be possible to read this chapter through the lens of beliefs. Instead, I want you to see it through the lens of the conscious commitments to choose to create what you most want. Commitment is the act of gathering yourself up and moving in a chosen direction. Commitment is the essential first step to create what you and your organization most want. Commitment and its cousin, recommitment, are the fuel that ignites transformation.

---

[61] Leveraging Polarities is the work of Barry Johnson of Polarity Partnerships, http://www.polaritypartnerships.com. I have studied "both/and" approaches with the Hendricks Institute, www. Hendricks.com.

Our commitments have an outsized role in the creation of our outcomes.

Here is an example of a commitment that I and many others have found valuable: I commit to taking full responsibility for my choices, feelings, expressions, and the circumstances of my life.

As Ari Weinzweig, CEO and co-founder of the Ann Arbor, Michigan-based Zingerman's gourmet food company, says, "Dig up the roots to get a new root system." If you have toxic roots—fear-driven beliefs or commitments—you must dig them up at the root and plant a new set of healthy, thriving roots to create new outcomes. Here is the challenge: toxic commitments may be so deeply embedded that you are not aware of them.

Let's look at some commitments you may want to trade in and upgrade:

Old Toxic Commitment	Conscious Commitment
I commit to experiencing life as hard.	I commit to seeing that the universe collaborates with me as I learn and grow.
I commit to seeing myself as the smartest person in the room.	I commit to discovery as my primary way of being.
I commit to making up what I think others are thinking.	I commit to speaking authentically as I create connection and resonance.

It's a big moment when you wake up to the reality that existing toxic commitments are running your life. It can be enlivening—and it can be terrifying. This kind of awareness will normally initiate one or more of the five core feelings. Let's explore them in greater detail with this question in mind: What am I doing in the gap between the opportunity to commit and committing?

The Five Core Feelings:

- Sad

- Angry

- Scared

- Joy

- Sexual

All other feelings are either a different intensity of one of these or a combination of several of these. Frustration? That's low-level anger. Rage? A more intense level of anger. Shame is a mixture of sadness, anger, and fear, with a story and experience mixed in.

The five core feelings naturally flow through our bodies intermittently on an ongoing basis, if we allow them to. However, from an early age, feelings often are not welcomed.

Have you seen a four-year-old fall over and attempt to stop their sadness by holding their breath? Their breath becomes shallow and jerky as they attempt to hold back their sadness and waves of tears. It's been drummed into them that they must suppress and control their emotions.

Observe a manager attempting to give feedback. They are often terrified the person receiving it will have an outburst of feelings. (Heaven forbid!) It's as if all the air is sucked out of the room—each person is barely breathing as they struggle to control their feelings. The big problem with this repeated behavior is feelings get stuck in our bodies.

There is growing scientific evidence that toxic emotions (those that get stuck in your body) contribute to disease—hence, dis-ease. But emotions are data packets intended to be supportive, not feared.

WHOLE-BODY WISDOM PRACTICES, PART ONE: LET YOUR FEELINGS FLOW

So let's look at some ways that you can practice allowing yourself to experience your feelings flowing.

Breathe to Create Flow:

The most reliable way to shift your physiology and inner experience when you feel stuck is to breathe. There are many formal ways to learn breathing and many resources to support you. Simply inhaling and allowing your relaxed belly to expand and then gently exhaling is a great start.

The Breathing Exercise:

Breathe in for a count of four seconds, allowing your belly to expand, then exhale for four seconds. (Make sure your clothes allow your belly to expand easily.)

Gently complete four full breathing cycles, which should take roughly half a minute.

Allow your body to relax and note if your shoulders are holding any tightness. Bring them up toward your ears, and then release, dropping your arms and shoulders like a dead weight.

What do you notice?

Some people might feel more relaxed, with less tightness. Others might notice they feel tired and start yawning. No matter what you experience, this is a simple and effective way to get present. Four complete breathing cycles have been shown to reset your physiology, which will create a measurable reduction in your stress response when you commit to practice regularly.

Practicing breathing for a couple of minutes first thing in the morning and the last thing at night can build your capacity to use breath as a "go to" shift move. Breathing into any feeling or sensation you are experiencing with your non-judgmental, preferably loving, attention allows the sensation to expand and dissipate. When your feelings start to flow, you may initially experience the sensation as "growing." However, as you continue to breathe with your feeling, the sensations will start to morph and dissipate. Don't take my word for it; try it out for yourself!

Movement Shifts:

Walking, moving, dancing, and playing sports are examples of great activities to generate flow, as long as your big brain is not creating some other triggering event. The additional beauty of movement is it requires breathing. So breathing and moving are the fundamental building blocks for transforming any stuck-ness, or uncomfortable body sensations and feelings. At the same time, they generate a feeling of aliveness and enjoyment.

Use the breath and movement practices (as well as any other shifts you already enjoy) to allow any and all of the five core feelings to flow.

WHOLE-BODY WISDOM PRACTICES, PART TWO: TRANSFORM FEAR - TRANSFORM THE PLANET

Let's focus some additional attention on the unique emotion of fear. It seems to be reaching epidemic proportions in organizations, and in life in general. Fear is corrosive when allowed to become habitualized; when we continually re-experience it. But it's not a problem to experience fear that is allowed to simply flow through your body. I want to address how to allow fear to flow so that it does not become toxic fear, which wreaks havoc when it gets trapped in people and organizations.

It's another reason why I think whole-body wisdom is essential for any individual or organization to grow: it gives you the tools to allow fear to flow.

I feel sad and angry as I watch adult professionals reduced to scared children day after day. I see people who simply want job security and the experience of being accepted, honored, and appreciated. They are looking to the outside world to create those experiences when they must be generated internally—it's an inside job, if you will. A great place to start is to ask if you love yourself unconditionally. If not, I invite you to start that journey and commit to loving yourself for the rest of your life. Without you loving yourself, you will never feel fully loved, and ultimately you won't feel safe, secure, and appreciated. You will be at the effect of yourself and others as you look for safety, security, and approval from others and futilely attempt to control your life and those around you.

While people experience fear, they often withhold important communications, don't ask for what they want, and become more and more embroiled in reactionary behaviors. This wastes your time, your energy, and your talent. Unexpressed and unfelt sadness, anger, and fear can build up. It is mind-boggling how we continue to make these choices. However, you can't take responsibility until you are "response-able"; that is, able to respond. Without the requisite understanding, knowledge, and practiced ability to allow your fear and other feelings to flow through you, it is not possible to build your response-agility capacity.

When I interview people for open positions, the *number one requirement* I'm looking for is the demonstrated ability to be open to discovery and learning. Any issue can be resolved when there's a shared commitment to discovery and learning. Major business disruption or new "competitors" in the marketplace? No problem. Natural disaster in the local area? No problem. Public company disgrace due to illegal behaviors in the company? No problem. There may be feelings and communications to process, but that can happen easily with awake and aware people.

Unfortunately, all too often, leaders are more committed to blocking feedback or learning. John Gottman, PhD., has researched the ways that people resist connection. He identified what he dubbed the "Four Horsemen of the Apocalypse"—the four behaviors that reliably create disconnection from self and others: criticism, contempt, defensiveness, and stonewalling. These keep us operating from a victim's mentality. They are attempts to distract us from what we are feeling. Underlying each of these four ways of acting out is the felt sense of fear.

There are several ways to recognize when you are experiencing fear. Physical sensations like butterflies in the stomach are an obvious tell, as is exhibiting any of the Four Horsemen behaviors listed above. We often experience fear as a sense of victimization, or we experience it mixed up with other core emotions like anger, which prevents us from recognizing the fear.

Kathlyn Hendricks has developed a practice she calls Fear Melters™.[62] They are a series of simple movements to

---

[62]   Fear Melters™ Kathlyn Hendricks created Fear Melters after having worked with thousands of clients and knowing that this was the skill that could change the way we interact with each other and our planet. YouTube animation shares more detail: https://www.youtube.com/watch?v=pGS2byt4kZ8&t=59s

move from fear to flow. When I teach people how to melt their fear, I first need to encourage them to be aware of the fact that they are scared—which at times is no easy feat.

Let's say you have recognized one of the above indicators that you are scared, and you want to melt your fear. You can start by recognizing which one or more of the four fear response/reactions you are having:

Fear Response/ Reactions	Fear Melters™
Freeze	**Wiggle** your toes and fingers, and then your whole body.
Flee	**Sumo** - Adopt a sumo posture, with legs planted wide, hands on your legs above your knees as you bend forward from the waist. Experience being grounded as you face what you are feeling, instead of fleeing.
Fight	**Ooze** - Imagine that you are ice cream and that warm fudge is being poured over you. Imagine your head, shoulders and back all melting with the warm fudge. You won't be able to hold onto your fight energy as you allow yourself to physically melt.
Faint - The experience of faint is when you get confused or scattered.	**Love Scoops** - Reach out in front of you and gather "loving scoops of energy" or appreciation. Gather the positive energy and gently bring it to your different body parts, like your heart, your head, and your gut.

To support your fear-melting practice, look for Fear Melter videos on YouTube.[63] When I visualize fear melting it reminds me of Dawn®, the dishwashing liquid used in toxic spills to disperse the oil in the ocean or clean coastal birds trapped in the spillage. When whole-body wisdom and shift moves are practiced, fear can simply melt away in moments. Yes, it takes practice. Commit to specific practices and keep doing them until they become your go-to calming resource.

A recent Gallup survey found that 70 percent of employees are not engaged or actively disengaged at work. How many times have you read that data point, which has barely shifted in thirty years? Unfortunately, "actively disengaged" employees can be actively engaged in sabotaging your organization. The good news: the impulse to sabotage drops away when organizations encourage people to maintain whole-body wisdom practices. Employees are more committed to an organization in which colleagues own their feelings, respond with agility, and make conscious commitments. Conversely, a person committed to negative behaviors finds that they can no longer coexist in a department or organization committed to conscious healthy behaviors. Either way, it leaves the organization in a better place.

I know that many people (myself included) get triggered by words. I understand that some of the terms used in this chapter may have inadvertently triggered some of you. Let's take "integrity." It can be interpreted as hectoring and moralistic. "Feelings" is another word that gets under the skin. Messiness, transformation, victimhood—just buzzwords and "woo-woo" stuff to many. I genuinely do not want to trigger you, and I understand this is not in my

---

63　Fear Melters™ YouTube animation shares more detail: https://www.youtube.com/watch?v=pGS2byt4kZ8&t=59s

"things I can control" file. I have delayed writing for many years as I did not want to offend, seem like a know-it-all, or articulate something poorly. As community activist and political news commentator Van Jones said, "Grow your goddamn comfort zone." That's good advice for everyone, myself included.

Einstein offered another useful bit of wisdom about exploring new things: "A problem cannot be solved from the same level of consciousness that created it."

If you feel triggered, feel free to own your experience, then take a chance. Select a shift move, breathe, change your posture, and start the journey to creating what you most want in life.

NEXT ACTION: PUTTING IT ALL TOGETHER

"An organization cannot grow beyond the consciousness of its leader." - Frederic Laloux

The power of leadership is ignited when we realize that we are both leaders and followers. When we choose to powerfully lead our lives and our work and follow others from our whole-body wisdom, anything is possible.

There is no myth of arrival. There will not be a day in the future where everything is permanently perfect. Well, let me contradict myself. You are "perfect" exactly as you are in this moment. You are a combination of all your life experiences; your current version and evolution are the outcome. You are totally lovable, however bad you secretly think you are. You may choose to focus on new beliefs and behaviors and increasing your response-agility quotient. I support you on that journey if that is your choice. If you do, my experience is that you will have more and more fun. That fun may come in the form of connection, or uncovering the real you, or the experience of living in integrity with yourself. It can be the fun of creating the positive impact you want to see, do, and be in the world.

When you are tapped into your whole-body wisdom, you will notice emergent thoughts. New connections will be made. Your intuition will come online like never before. All that creativity will require a whole new system to be able to process your new level of flow and innovative thoughts. That will happen whether you are an accountant, a compliance officer, a designer, or dancer.

The more you focus on your WBW, the more you will be in flow with the universe and increase your creativity. You may even come up with the next amazing thing the world wants, like Zoom, Expensify, Patagonia, Numi Tea, Eileen Fisher, REI, or EO Products (all my personal favorites).

* Transformation is about simple practices—noticing what you are thinking, feeling, and experiencing. I invite you to see your data packets as gifts from the universe that emerge minute to minute, sent to guide you to what you most want, to your innate talents, to aligned decisions, and to ripplicious impact.

I experience joy, knowing I have an internal data bank providing me with stellar research and data 24/7. I can pull a report down in seconds. I am simply required to commit to the following:

- I want to know what I am thinking, feeling, and experiencing.

- I'm willing to know what I am thinking, feeling, and experiencing.

- I commit to know what I am thinking, feeling, and experiencing.

- I re-commit to know what I am thinking, feeling, and experiencing.

These practices reliably open a channel to connect authentically with yourself. Your presence then opens up the possibility for greater creativity and collaboration. By expanding your whole-body wisdom capacity and response-agility quotient, you will be able to navigate the unknown, and that is very much needed now. We all know technological advances are not slowing.

No matter how intense, scary, and/or anger-inducing the situation is, if you have the body intelligence skills of noticing, breathing, moving, playing, fear-melting, and sharing authentically (and there are countless others), you will be able to create what you want while living in integrity. You will embody your purpose and contribute greatly to your organization's healthy culture and sustainable success.

CREATE A GREAT WORK CULTURE

The Great Work Cultures movement got started through the initiative of Joan Blades, a prominent activist for positive change, who attracted a network of people passionate about designing better workplaces. The GWC is making a difference by writing and speaking to audiences who are hungry for a better way. This book is an outcome of our intention to accelerate positive change at work.

Whether you're an entrepreneur looking for your first round of funding, a small business owner desperate for growth, or a manager at a global company performing below its potential, knowing how to create a great work culture is imperative if you want to succeed.

This book is written for leaders who want to do the best thing for all their stakeholders; their people, their clients, and their community. By writing this book, we hope to activate and provoke interest in leading the transformation to collaborative, networked organizations that value human experience over bureaucratic rule.

Engage and Share Your Results

To get started, Bill Sanders offers three steps you can take to support your efforts to understand and help create the future of work.

- Address your view of adversity and failure
- Educate yourself on the trends, tools, and principles
- Experiment and take risks

We collectively offer a fourth:

- Engage and share your results.

Join us at http://www.greatworkcultures.org/join to connect with us and share your results in applying these recommendations and principles. We look forward to working with you for a better future.

GWC BIOS AND PHOTOS

Bill Sanders is the founder and managing director of Roebling Strauss, Inc., a boutique consultancy that specializes in delivering dramatic improvements in organizational effectiveness and innovation. An organizational process expert, Bill uses his proven holistic approach to rapidly identify misalignments between strategy, goals, process and execution, and then designs elegant solutions that close those gaps, accelerating growth, profitability and innovation. Bill's expertise has attracted over 200 organizations including such global brands as Google, Microsoft, PepsiCo, General Mills, Lipton, Hewlett-Packard, and WebEx.

Dawna Jones provides insights accompanied by advanced decision-making awareness for clarity, greater accuracy and increased responsiveness especially in complex environments.

Her transformational insights free personal and organizational potential to be more creatively responsive to high-speed change. Speaker, author, strategist and educator. Author of *Decision Making for Dummies*, contributor to *The Intelligence of the Cosmos*, and host of the *Insight to Action* podcast. Dawna works to connect decision-making leadership to restore ecological and social – economic health led by business and consumers in partnership.

Ozlem Brooke Erol started her career at IBM. After her own journey to figure out what her purpose in life is, she started her first business, Your Best Life Inc., in 2003 (www.yourbestlifeinc.com) to help professionals have more fulfilling careers. After being around so many unhappy people at work, her new business (www.Purposeful.Business) helps leaders create inspiring and purpose-driven environments. She is the author of *Create a Life You Love*, and co-author of *Transform Your Life II*.

Josh Levine is an educator, designer, and author, but above all, he is on a mission to help organizations design a culture advantage. Even though his day job is Principal of Great Monday, a 10-year-old culture design company, Josh is most known as a co-founder of the international non-profit Culture LabX in 2013. His book Great Mondays: How To Design a Company Culture Employees Love is available on Amazon. You can find him around the web @ akajoshlevine. www.akajoshlevine.com.

Sue Bingham, founder and principal of HPWP Group, has been at the forefront of the positive business movement for 35 years. She's driven to create high performing workplaces by partnering with courageous leaders who value the contributions of team members. She is the author of *Creating the High-performance Work Place: It's Not Complicated to Develop a Culture of Commitment.*

Doug Kirkpatrick is an organizational change consultant, TEDx and keynote speaker, blogger, educator, executive coach, dual citizen and author of *Beyond Empowerment: The Age of the Self-Managed Organization.* He engages with Great Work Cultures, LeadWise, Center for Innovative Cultures and other communities to co-create the future of work. Doug enjoys travel in rough parts of the world and appreciates the perspective he gains from it.

Since 2003, **Anna McGrath** has supported organizations globally to build response-agility into their cultures and transition into self-organizing structures. She has worked with the full continuum of organizations, from traditional hierarchies to bleeding-edge start-ups, and is a popular speaker on Holacracy™, transformation, and whole-body wisdom practices. After 14 years of incubation and experimentation, her company, WonderWorks Consulting, was acquired by Godfrey Dadich Partners, where Anna is currently Partner, Culture and Transformation.

34673384R00074

Printed in Poland
by Amazon Fulfillment
Poland Sp. z o.o., Wrocław